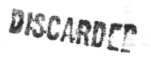

The Philosophical Disenfranchisement of Art

The Philosophical Disenfranchisement of Art

Arthur C. Danto

Columbia University Press

New York   1986

Columbia University Press
New York   Guildford, Surrey
Copyright © 1986 Columbia University Press

Library of Congress Cataloging-in-Publication Data

Danto, Arthur Coleman, 1924–
   The philosophical disenfranchisement of art.

   1. Aesthetics—Addresses, essays, lectures.
2. Art—Philosophy—Addresses, essays, lectures.
I. Title.
BH39.D35   1986   700'.1   86-2260
ISBN 0-231-06364-4

This book is Smyth-sewn.

Book design by J. S. Roberts

For Barbara Westman

Contents

Preface

ONCE, IN AN exhibition of conceptual art held at the New York Cultural Center, I saw a work consisting of an ordinary table with some books on it. The books themselves were by analytical philosophers such as Wittgenstein and Carnap, Ayer and Reichenbach, Tarski and Russell. It could have been a table in my study, since it was sufficiently nondescript to be reduced to a mere working surface, and the books were of the sort I consulted frequently in the sort of philosophical work I was then doing.

That there should be a work of art which looked, for every relevant purpose, like an object out of the *Lebenswelt*, with no claim whatever to the status of art, was a possibility already well understood. Certainly it was well understood by me, since it was precisely that possibility that generated my own first efforts at the philosophy of art. My first paper, "The Artworld" of 1964, had been an analytical response to an exhibition to which I have often referred, consisting of effigies of Brillo cartons by Andy Warhol, held at the Stable Gallery earlier that year. The question of why these were art while Brillo cartons, which they pretty closely resembled, were not, was the problem that possessed me then. It was clear that the differences between an ordinary Brillo box and one of Warhol's could not account for the difference between art and reality, and the question was what can.

By 1964, Abstract Expressionism was doomed as an art movement, and indeed its dismantling began as early as 1957 through the work of Johns and Rauschenberg, who used some of its forms to disguise the fact that they had begun something new and incompatable with its own preoccupations and premisses. But it was still vital in the minds of a great many artists, and I recall the violent repudiation of the ideas I set forth in "The Artworld" when I presented them, at the invitation of the critic Irving Sandler, at "The Club," as it was called: a place where painters of the second generation of Abstract Expressionism met for rowdy disputations. Artists were clearly not ready for a philosophy of art which put no premium whatever on the romantic and gestural imperatives that defined painting for members of The Club, all of whose backs were against the wall, though few then realized it. The only sympathy I received that evening was from the painter Al Held, himself already changing artistic directions: he led me, like Virgil, past the howling and voluble men and women who did not want to hear what I had to say.

But when philosophical books of the austere and technical order of those laid out on that table began, as it were, to be preempted by the artworld and made its own, it was as though some deep transformation in artistic consciousness had taken place. A wholly different relationship between philosophy and art, a mere decade after the debacle at the Club, now seemed to exist. It was, almost, as if philosophy were somehow now part of the artworld, a fact for which this work was a metaphor, whereas in 1964 philosophy stood outside that world and addressed it from across an alienating distance. Who can forget Barnett Newman's cruel *boutade*, flung at, of all people, Susanne Langer: "Aesthetics is for art what ornithology is for the birds"? Now it was as though art were beckoning to philosophy to articulate a relationship such works as the one showing books on a table could but symbolize.

One philosophical consequence of there being works of art exactly like the most ordinary of used objects was that the difference between them could not rest on any presumed aesthetic difference. Aesthetic qualities had once seemed to theorists to be sufficiently like sense qualities as to suggest that the sense of beauty should be a seventh sense—with moral sensibility perhaps a sixth sense. But just as the artwork and the real thing shared all sensory qualities, so that we could not tell them apart on the basis of the senses alone, neither could we tell them apart aesthetically, if aesthetic differences were like sense differences. It is *not* that aesthetics is irrelevant to the appreciation of art, but only that it cannot be part of the definition of art if one of the purposes of the definition is to explain in what way artworks differ from real things. That differentiation was what I pursued through a series of writings which culminated in *The Transfiguration of the Commonplace*. One of the components it seemed to me must be central to the identity of works of art was their historical location. That is, something being the work it was, or even being a work of art at all, was a partial function of where in the historical order it originated, and with which other works it could be situated in the historical complex to which it belonged. History, and art history in particular, was then not something that provides interesting but largely external facts about works already fully accessible without knowledge of those facts. The familiar image of the historically ignorant viewer transfixed by the timeless power of artworks had to be abandoned. There was no timeless power. So one pole in my analysis was that historical circumstance penetrates the substance of art, so that two indiscriminable objects from different historical periods would or could be vastly different as works of art, with different structures and meanings, and calling for different responses. In order to respond to them at all, an interpretation constrained by the limits of historical possibility was required. History, in brief, because it was inseparable from interpretation, was inseparable from art itself just because artworks themselves are internally related to the interpretations that define them.

So history has a role to play in the philosophical analysis of art. So much I recognized, but I cannot pretend to have begun to think about what one might call the philosophical structure of the history of art until that table of philosophy books provided the stimulus. If art should at one stage reject philosophy as "for the birds" and at a later stage demand philosophy as part of its substance, then one has almost an illustration of what Hegel thought of as stages in the history of Spirit, which culminates in the advent of Spirit attaining to a philosophical understanding of its own nature. When Spirit, as subject, grasps the essence of Spirit, as object—when subject and object become one—a gap will have been closed and a period of internal development will have run its course. These are extravagant ideas, to be sure, but they provoked me to develop a philosophy of the history of art, rather than rest content with a philosophy of art with an ineliminable historical dimension. And of course, since the philosophy of history suggested by Hegel requires that philosophy emerge at a certain point in the historical process, what I was trying to think about was also required to be a philosophy of the philosophy of art.

Anyone who has kept close to the artworld, especially the New York artworld, through the past several decades—my own connection to it began in the late 1940s—has to be aware of the extraordinary swings and shifts that punctuate its chronicle. Abstract Expressionism rose to world prominence through the 1950s only to end, abruptly, in the next decade. As the stubborn resistances of the members of The Club testify, the ideologies of Abstract Expressionism continued to dominate artistic thought about art long past the point where the movement it defined was the creative edge of art history. Something alien to it, whose premisses would be unthinkable to Expressionism, was already beginning to take its place. This was Pop Art, irreverent and cerebral. And then, after the mid-sixties and on through the 1970s, one movement succeeded another so rapidly that it seemed as if the history of art was a concatenation of novelties. Surely there would have been in this some occasion for reflection: was there any order to art history, any internal necessity, as it were, which was driving art forward? After all, the succession of movements could be perceived virtually as moments in a continuing conversation. Or was it in fact just one thing after another, with no internal or development core?

For me, this question became vivid in the early 1980s, when a curious movement began to arouse immense enthusiasm on the part of dealers and collectors, curators and critics, with a wide participation of young artists. This was Neo-Expressionism, which burst into the consciousness of the artworld after over a decade of what retrospectively seemed stagnation, when there was no particular direction to be discerned, but simply the ceaseless modification of existing forms and styles, minimal perturbations of the already accepted and already understood, where the only available or justifiable ideology seemed to be a kind of benign pluralism: do whatever you like. Since everything was on the same footing as everything else—Realism, Abstraction, Expressionism, Minimalism—there could be no room for breakthrough. But now, abruptly, here is Neo-Expressionism, deliriously hailed as breakthrough after all. The history of art was back on its tracks! It was heading somewhere at last! Of course this awakened a nostalgia for earlier excitements. It was like the forties, the fifties, the sixties, all over again. There was the accompanying sense that the future would be even finer, and having learned how valuable as an investment art can become, there was competition to get in on the ground floor, to buy while the buying was possible. It was my conviction that this picture of history was false. I thought: art does not have that kind of future.

There was a moment when this thought struck me with

the force of a revelation. I was standing in one of the Whitney Biennials, looking at some of the new slurried canvases, immense and bombastic, puerile and portentous, shallow and brash. This, I thought, was not the way things were supposed to go next, and with that it seemed to me that art must after all have an ordered history, a way in which things have to go rather than some other way. Art history must have an internal structure and even a kind of necessity. This was the conviction that motivated my essay "The End of Art," and the other writings which undertake to articulate a philosophy of the history of art in exactly the grand manner I had learned from Hegel, and which it astonished me that I was accepting, since my first book, the *Analytical Philosophy of History* of 1965, had pretty much taken a stand against its possibility in principle. Right or wrong, my view now was that the artworld was not demanding only a philosophy of art. It was demanding a philosophy of its own history. And it is that that the essays which compose the present volume mean to lay out.

Written for different occasions, the nine essays collected here develop themes set forth in this introduction. They attempt to explain the theses about art and interpretation, art and philosophy, and about art and historical consciousness. They do not constitute everything I have written on these subjects, or in general on the philosophy of art since the publication, in 1982 of *The Transfiguration of the Commonplace.* And they exclude the art criticism I have been writing for *The Nation* since 1984. But they form a natural narrative order, almost as though they were chapters in a single book with an overarching theme. Each stands on its own as an integral essay, but even so it is best to read them from beginning to end, as if the beginning and end of a single philosophical story.

The story begins with two disenfranchising movements, aggressions, really, made against art by philosophy. The first is the effort to ephemeralize art by treating it as fit only for pleasure, and the second is the view that art is just philosophy in an alienated form: what it requires, as it were, is only an awakening kiss in order to recognize that it really was philosophy all along, only bewitched. Both disenfranchisements are in Plato's philosophy of art—they *are* Plato's philosophy of art—and my essays seek a reenfranchisement against both moves. The first set of countermoves explicates the relationship between art and interpretation, and in particular seek to make aesthetic consideration secondary in the appreciation of works of art. The second set tries to force an essential division between philosophy and art, which then breaks the connection between them that has generated the model of art history in which art comes to its end and fulfillment in its own philosophical self-consciousness. My aim is to show that we have entered a period of post-historical art, where the need for constant self-revolutionization of art is now past. There can and should never again be anything like the astonishing sequence of convulsions that have defined the art history of our century. Of course there will always be external causes for making it appear as though such a history must go on and on, preeminently the externalities of the art market itself, which thrives on the illusion of unending novelty. Such an appearance will be shown to be artifactual and contrived, and essentially empty. In a sense, the post-historical atmosphere of art will return art to human ends. The fermentation of the twentieth century will prove to have been terminal, but exciting as it has been to live through it, we are entering a more stable, more happy period of artistic endeavor where the basic needs to which art has always been responsive may again be met.

The book is dedicated to my wife, Barbara Westman, a person of overwhelming cheer, celebration, and creativity. She is my paradigm as well of the post-historical artist. My intellectual and artistic debts cannot be discharged here, but I owe particular gratitude to Richard Kuhns and David Carrier, with whom the central arguments and theses of the book have been discussed. Ben Sonnenberg, creator and edi-

tor of the magazine *Grand Street*, has gotten me to move in
novel directions as one who thinks and writes about art.
Columbia University Press has been remarkably hospitable
in taking this book on: I am grateful to John Moore and
William Germano for their enthusiasm, and to Maureen
MacGrogan for her warm and generous support. I have
greatly benefited from conversations with Arakawa and
Madeline Gins, and am in Arakawa's debt for allowing the
use of his drawing for the jacket.

The Philosophical Disenfranchisement of Art

I.

The Philosophical Disenfranchisement of Art

I am learning that it's inspiriting to be
where writers can be dangerous.
        —Hortense Calisher

This essay is an expanded version of a plenary address before the World Congress of Aesthetics, in Montreal, August 1984. The theme of that conference was "Art and the Transformations of Philosophy." A slightly modified version appeared in Grand Street. *I am grateful to Professor Elinor West for her deep analyses of the relationship between Plato and Aristophanes. If she is right, we read an impoverished text of the Republic in not appreciating the punning references to Aristophanes the original readers of such texts would have been alive to.*

IN HIS GREAT poem on the death of William Butler Yeats, Auden wrote: "Ireland has her madness and her weather still/ For poetry makes nothing happen." No one, I suppose, not even a poetic visionary, would have expected lyrics to dispel the humidities of the Emerald Isle, and this gives Auden his paradigm of artistic impotency. The equation with Ireland's political madness is then meant to discourage the comparably futile but more often held hope that the right bit of verse *might* make something happen—though it is not to the especial discredit of art that it is ineffective in Irish politics, where it is not plain that anything else could be effective. "I think it better that in times like these / A poet's mouth be silent, for in truth / We have no gift to set a statesman right," Yeats wrote as a poetic refusal to write a War Poem. And he seems to have endorsed the thought Auden expressed to the extent of dignifying as art failed political actions, if fervently enough motivated: "We know their dream; enough / To know they dreamed and are dead; / And what if excess of love / Bewildered them till they died? . . . A terrible beauty is born." That politics becomes poetry when enobled by failure is a sentimental transfer I doubt would be consoling to the wild gunmen of the Easter Rising, since to be seriously enough bent on political change to spill real blood is exactly not to want one's actions appreciated merely as a kind of deflected writing in the medium of violence. To have slipped out of the order of effectiveness into the order of art, to have inadvertently achieved something of a piece with the golden bird in the Byzantine throne room or the unconnecting figure on the Grecian urn, must then be a doubled failure for the already defeated warrior.

"I know," Auden wrote, with his characteristic and endearing honesty, "that all the verse I wrote, all the positions I took in the thirties, did not save a single Jew. Those attitudes, those writings, only help oneself." And in a manuscript he worked on at the time of his marriage to Chester Kallman, we read:

Artists and politicians would get along better at a time of crisis like the present, if the latter would only realize that the political history of the world would have been the same if not a poem had been written, nor a picture painted, nor a bar of music composed.

This of course is an empirical claim, and it is difficult, simply because of difficulties in the topic of historical explanation, to know how true it is. Did jazz in any sense cause or only emblemize the moral transformations of the Jazz Age? Did the Beatles cause or only prefigure the political perturbations of the sixties—or had politics simply become a form of art in that period, at least the politics responsive to music, the real political history of the world taking place on a different level of causation? In any case, as we know, even works intended to prick consciousness to political concern have tended by and large to provoke at best an admiration for themselves and a moral self-admiration for those who admired them. The cynical bombing of the Basque village of Guernica on April 26, 1937, made *Guernica* happen—so it was not merely wit when Picasso responded to the German officer's question, having handed him a postcard of the painting, "Did you do that?" with "No, you did." Everyone knew who did what and why: it was an atrocity meant to be perceived as an atrocity by perpetrators who meant to be perceived as prepared to stop at nothing. The painting was used as a fundraiser for Spanish war relief, but those who paid money for the privilege of filing past it only used it as a mirror to reflect attitudes *already* in place, and in later years it required art-historical knowledge to know what was going on: it stood as a handsome backdrop for pickups at the Museum of Modern Art, or a place to meet a date, like the clock at the Biltmore Hotel, and it was sufficiently handsome in its grey and black harmonies to have ornamented the kitchen cupboard in a sophisticated apartment I once saw written up, where soufflées were concocted for bright and brittle guests who, no more than the hostess, realized that gutted animals and screaming mothers agonized above the formica: it was painted at about the same time as *Night Fishing at Antibes,* after all, as Anita Silvers has observed, and uses the same sorts of forms as that lyrical work. So in the end it did about as much for the ravaged villagers as Auden's poem did for dead Yeats or as Yeats' poem did for his slaughtered patriots, making nothing relevant happen, simply memorializing, enshrining, spiritualizing, constituting a kind of cenotaph to house the fading memories, about at the level of a religious ceremony whose function is to confess the extreme limitation of our powers to make anything happen. Hegel places religion just next to art in the final stages of the itinerary of the Spirit, where history is done with and there is nothing left but to become conscious of what in any case cannot be changed.

Fine. But if the sole political role of poetry is this deflected, consolatory, ceremonial—not to say reliquary—office, why is it so widely subscribed a political attitude that *art is dangerous*? The history of art is the history of the suppression of art, itself a kind of futility if that which one seeks to cast in chains has no effectiveness whatever, and one confers upon art the illusion of competence by treating as dangerous what would make nothing happen if it were allowed to be free. Where, if Auden is right, does the belief in the dangerousness of art come from? My own view, which I mean to develop in this essay, is that it does not come from historical knowledge, but rather from a philosophical belief. It is based upon certain theories of art that philosophers have advanced, whatever it may be that caused them in the first place so to have sensed a danger in art that the history of philosophy itself might almost be regarded as a massive collaborative effort to neutralize an activity. Indeed, construing art, as Auden does, as a causally or politically neutered activity is itself an act of neutralization. Representing art as something that in its nature can make nothing happen is not so much a view opposed to the view that art is dangerous: it is a way of responding to the sensed danger of art by treating it metaphysically as though there were nothing to be afraid of.

Now it is my thought that we cannot arrive at an assessment of what art is nor what art can and cannot do, nor where in the political plane its natural locus is, until we have archeologized these disenfranchising theories. The relationship of art to philosophy is ancient and intricate, and though I shall paint it in very lurid terms, here and throughout this book, I am obliged to acknowledge that its sublety may transcend our powers of analytical depiction, much as the relationship of mind to body does, since it is far from plain that we can separate art from philosophy, inasmuch as its substance is in part constituted by what it is philosophically believed to be. And its insubstantiation by its oppressor may be one of the great victories of political metaphysics.

In the first serious philosophical writings on art—perhaps the first writings in which art is so much as recognized as such—a kind of warfare between philosophy and art is declared. Inasmuch as philosophy itself is a warring discipline, in which philosophy is divided against philosophy with nearly the degree of antagonism we find expressed between philosophy and art in the fateful initiating pages of platonic aesthetics, it ought to be cause for suspicion that there is a near unanimity on the part of philosophers of art that art makes nothing happen: for on what else do philosophers agree? Even so engaged a writer as Sartre thought of art, hence thought of his own practice as a novelist in the fiction in which he sets forth this view, as lying outside the order of existential contingencies: a shelter against mutability. Plato notoriously identified the practice of art with the creation of appearances of appearances, twice removed from the reality philosophy addresses. It is striking that Sartre, like Keats, like Yeats, puts artistic reality exactly where Plato put philosophical reality, but this interchange leaves the topology unaltered, and we may remark anticipatorily at this point that the charge that *philosophy* makes nothing happen is not unfamiliar. In any case, both philosophy and art, on the platonic scheme, contrast with the kind of practical knowledge possessed by craftspeople, whose products artists merely imitate. And Plato seized upon the inference that one can imitate without possessing the slightest knowledge of what one imitates save how it appears, so that if what one imitates is knowledge, it is consistent that one can appear to have it while lacking it altogether. It is important for Plato to quarantine art against the practico-political sphere in which the philosopher may deign to descend (himself imitating the relationship in which Forms stand to appearances), and the thought that art is arrested in the realm of second-order appearances assures that it can make nothing happen in even the slightly less degenerate realm of first-order appearances, being radically epiphenomenal, like a dream or a shadow or a mere reflection. It is as though platonic metaphysics was generated in order to define a place for art from which it is then a matter of cosmic guarantee that nothing can be made by it to happen.

It is more or less for these reasons that I have diagnosed Plato's theory of art as largely political, a move in some struggle for domination over the minds of men in which art is conceived of as the enemy. So the portrait of the artist we get in Book Ten of *The Republic* has to be placed alongside the portrait of the philosopher—the portrait in fact of Socrates—we get in Aristophanes's cruel comedy, *The Clouds,* where the philosopher is stigmatized for being out of touch with the same reality Plato stigmatizes the artist as capable only of imitating. *The Clouds* is an attack on intellect in the name of feeling, much in the way, millennia later, Lawrence is going to celebrate feeling against Russell, whom he fictionalizes in *St. Maur* with aristophanic malice. So it is only taking art at its own self-estimate when Socrates explains to the rhapsode, Ion, that he (characteristic of his discipline) lacks knowledge, his powers being not those of reason but of darker and more confused forces which overcome Ion and ultimately swamp an audience itself addressed at a level lower than intellect so far as it succumbs. And Ion is depicted as stupid by Plato in order to dramatize a confirmation of the psychology of *The Republic,* art being used against art in sly duplicity. And Plato, as metaphysical politician, extrudes the artist both from republic and from reality, to which he is so loosely tethered that imitation gives us less a theory than a powerfully disabling metaphor for impotency. The combination of danger and ineffectiveness sounds contradictory until we recognize that the latter is a philosophical response to the former, for if art can be transferred ontologically to the sphere of secondary and derivative entities—shadows, illusions, delusions, dreams, mere appearances, and sheer reflections—well, this is a brilliant way to put art out of harm's way if we can get people to accept a picture of the world in which the place of art is outside it. And since Plato's theory of art *is* his philosophy, and since philosophy down the ages has consisted in placing codicils to the platonic testament, philosophy itself may just be the disenfranchisement of art—so the problem of separating art from philosophy may be matched by the problem of asking what philosophy would be without art.

There are two stages to the platonic attack. The first, just sketched, is to put across an ontology in which reality is logically immunized against art. The second stage consists so far as possible in rationalizing art, so that reason bit by bit colonizes the domain of feelings, the socratic dialogue being a form of dramatic representation in which the substance is reason exhibited as taming reality by absorbing it into concepts. Nietzsche refers to this as "aesthetic socratism," the philosopher having so identified reason with beauty that nothing could be beautiful that is not rational. This, Nietzsche proposes, marks the death of tragedy, which finds a terrible beauty in irrationality: but it also marks the death of comedy, which Socrates assures us comes to the same thing. And ever since this complex aggression, as profound a victory as philosophy has ever known or ever will know, the history of philosophy has alternated between the analytical effort to ephemeralize and hence defuse art, or, to allow a degree of validity to art by treating it as doing what philosophy itself does, only uncouthly.

This latter, hegelian strategy then raises the question of what it is that philosophy does—after all, philosophy stands just next to religion and art in his scheme—and there is a comic justice in the fact that the two-stage attack consisting of ephemeralization and takeover has characterized the sorry history of philosophy in recent times—as though it after all had but consisted in the weapons it was destined to die from. In the period of high positivism, for example, philosophy was cast in a role relative to science parallel to that in which art was placed relative to philosophical knowledge in the platonic scheme—so distant from the cognizable, not to say meaningful, order of things that "philosophy makes nothing happen" follows as a matter of course. "Philosophy begins when language goes on holiday" is a wittgensteinian echo of the invidious contrast between artmaking and the real skills of carpentry and navigation, with philosophy now the useless shadow of serious endeavor. And it became a metaphilosophical consensus that since there is no body of fact for philosophy to deal with alongside the body of fact—the World—which science addresses, the problems of philosophy only appear to be real problems but are actually nonsense, or *Scheinsprobleme*. Professor Rorty's deconstruction carries this sour assessment into the immediate moment. But now comes the consoling thought that to the degree that it had any validity at all, philosophy tried to do what science really does, just as Plato had said in effect that art did poorly what philosophy does well: philosophy just *is* impatient science. Caught in the dilemma of being either pseudo-science or proto-science, philosophy thus reenacts the dilemma Plato set for art. And perhaps if we could liberate philosophy from these toils we might find no better place to begin than liberating art from them, and by emancipating art from its philosophy we might emancipate philosophy from its own parallel philosophy: the liberation of the oppressed being, by a familiar liberationist formula, the liberation of the oppressor as well. In any case there must be something deeply common to two enterprises which seem subject to a common dissolution, especially when this form of dissolution has no obvious application elsewhere, unless (of course) to religion. Before addressing myself to these last optimisms, let me somewhat confirm my brash historical claims on the phi-

losophy of art by considering the two forms of repression—
what I refer to as ephemeralization and takeover—as exhibited in the unsuspecting thought of Kant and Hegel. The texts
of course are familiar—but the political subtexts are perhaps
not.

For Kant, to begin with, our attitude toward works of art
is characterized in terms of what he calls *disinterest,* itself an
attitude with which an immediate contrast exists with having an interest, hence some personal or social reason for
caring whether or not something exists, since its not existing,
or even its changing in certain ways, would make some individual or social difference. With works of art we have nothing of this sort to gain or lose. It is not difficult to see how
Kant should take this view, given the systematic constraints
of his philosophy, for what he was concerned to show was
that aesthetic judgments are universal, with which having an
interest would somehow be incompatible: if my judgment is
contaminated with my interests, it hardly could claim an
acquiescence of those whose interests differ. One of the reasons Plato thought philosophers should be kings was that
they, concerned only and ultimately with pure forms, could
not coherently *have* any intersts in the world of appearances,
hence not be motivated by what normally move men and
women—money, power, sex, love—and so could achieve disinterested decisions. Plato cleverly situates works of art outside the range of interests as well, since who could feel exultant at possessing what merely appeared to be gold? Since to
be human is very largely to have interests, art stands outside
the human order pretty much as reality stands outside the
primary apparent order in Plato's system—so though they
approach the issue from opposite directions, the implication
in both is that art is a kind of ontological vacation place from
our defining concerns as human, and with respect to which
accordingly "makes nothing happen." This is reinforced in
Kant when he speaks of art in terms of "purposiveness with-

out any specific purpose." The work of art looks as though it ought to be useful for something, but in philosophical truth it is not, and its logical purposelessness connects with the disinterestedness of its audience, since any use it might be put to would be a misuse, or a perversion. So art is systematically neutered, removed from the domain of use on one side (a good thing if artists lack practical intelligence they merely can give the appearance of having) and, on the other side, from the world of needs and interests. Its worth consists in its worthlessness, which you may recall is also Plato's caricature of the thought that justice is a skill: when would we *use* it?

Schopenhauer had a considerably higher regard for art than any Plato shows in his philosophy, but in an important sense he agrees with his great predecessors in agreeing that art makes nothing happen in the causal order of the world. Its importance rather consists in its power to lift us *out* of that order and to put us in a state of contemplation of eternal things. There is a characteristically bad inference that contemplation of the timeless is itself timeless, which then provides a lever for hoisting us, in fulfillment of a yeatsian wish, outside the order of time and suffering. We must appreciate that simply to exist in the causal stream is, on Schopenhauer's view, to suffer, since suffering is the defining trait of worldly existence. But then, one might parenthetically observe, one must distinguish between the sort of suffering in which the standard human condition simply consists, and that sort of suffering which occurs, say, to persecuted Jews and which Auden laments the incapacity of his poetry to mitigate. It certainly would have been a bitter counsel to suggest to the skeletal sufferers of Dachau that life *is* suffering, though the contemplation of art helps. As Auden once wrote on the particular issue of Third World hunger: "It's heartless to forget about / The underdeveloped countries, / But a starving ear is as deaf as a suburban optimist's." But I am less concerned to deal with the after all cheerful pessimism old Schopenhauer stood for than in stressing his continuity with Kant in locating art at right angles to the world as will.

Kant did suppose art should give pleasure, but it will have to be a disinterested pleasure, hence a tepid gratification since unconnected with the satisfaction of real needs or the achievement of real goals. So it is a kind of narcoleptic pleasure, the pleasure which consists in the absence of pain, which is just Schopenhauer's thought that the value of art must lie in the freedom it promises from topical urgencies in real life. Nevertheless, disinterested pleasure, with its implied contrast with the practical dimensions of lived existence, largely summarizes the manner in which philosophers of art have thought about art in the intervening years. Santayana thinks of art in terms of beauty and beauty in terms of objectified pleasure, which is to say pleasure contemplated rather than felt. Bullough keeps art at an aesthetic distance, drawing an explicit contrast between aesthetic and practical attitudes, our relationship to art beginning when practice goes on holiday. What Bullough calls aesthetic distance, other philosophers have spoken of as disinterested attention (Stolnitz) or intransitive perception (Vivas), which consists in looking at an object for no reason. And, to bring us to the threshold of the present discussion, Professor Dickie builds into his definition of art the condition that something must be in candidacy for appreciation—where he must clearly mean aesthetic appreciation, whatever his disclaimers, since he speaks of the chaste pleasure the eye might take in the curvatures and colors of an object—a urinal—which is not commonly appreciated for such reasons by those who primarily appreciate them.

This thumbnail runthrough of the table of contents of the standard undergraduate anthology of aesthetics yields an answer to the question anyone—a philistine, say—might wish to raise about art (testimony philosophers might offer when the National Endowment of the Arts comes under fire), namely what *good* art is, what *use* art has: its goodness consists in its not being good for anything, and its use consists in having none, so the question is misapplied. So that poetry makes nothing happen flows from the philosophical status assigned by philosophy to art: and this is a matter of such overwhelming philosophical consensus that it ought to give us pause. It leads us to wonder whether, rather than art being something the philosopher finally deals with in the name of and for the sake of systematic completeness—a finishing touch to an edifice—art is the reason philosophy was invented, and philosophical systems are finally penetentiary architectures it is difficult not to see as labyrinths for keeping monsters in and so protecting us against some deep metaphysical danger. And perhaps we ought to ask whether this war with which the discussion begins is not, millennia afterward, still being fought by philosophers who compete in ingenuity to the common end of putting out of play what they have not paused to wonder may not be an enemy at all? If each philosophical period requires a kind of booster, ought we not to ask ourselves at last what power it finally is that philosophy is afraid of? Perhaps the fear is that if the enemy is illusory, *philosophy* is illusory, since its prime objective has been to slay what only seems a dragon!

Indeed, it has at times struck me that the conventional division between the fine and the practical arts—between *les beaux arts* and *les arts pratiques*— serves, in the name of a kind of exaltation, to segregate *les beaux arts* from life in a manner curiously parallel to the way in which calling woman the *fair* sex is an institutional way of putting woman at an aesthetic distance—on a kind of moral pedestal which extrudes her from a world it is hoped she has no longer any business in. The power to classify is the power to dominate, and these parallel aestheticizations must be regarded as essentially political responses to what were sensed as dark dangers in both (see Germaine Greer). Aesthetics is an eighteenth-century invention, but it is exactly as political, and for the same causes, as Plato's was of setting artists at a distance for which *aesthetic* distance is a refined metaphor. It was a bold and finally successful strategy, leaving serious artists to suppose it their task to make beauty. So the metaphysical pedestal upon which art gets put—consider the museum as labyrinth—is a political translocation as savage as that which turned women into ladies, placing them in parlors doing things that seemed like purposive labor without specific purpose—viz., embroidery, watercolor, knitting: essentially frivolous beings, there for an oppressor's pleasure disguised as disinterested. Small wonder that Barnett Newman should have written in 1948: "The impulse of modern art was this desire to destroy beauty . . . by completely denying that art has any concern with the problem of beauty." Small wonder that Duchamp should have said, regarding his most famous work, "The danger to be avoided lies in aesthetic delectation:"

I owe to Duchamp the thought that from the perspective of art aesthetics is a danger, since from the perspective of philosophy *art* is a danger and aesthetics the agency for dealing with it. But then what should art be if it throws off the bondage to prettiness? It is not enough to be self-assertively ugly, though this is a tactic a good bit of recent art has sought to employ. Uglification is too negative a stance, and finally futile, since being ugly remains a way of being an aesthetic object and hence underscores bondage instead of overthrowing it. It is like the self-defeminization of women, casting frills to the flames. The way to stop being a sexual object is not to become an antisexual object, since one remains an *object* through that transformation when the problem is how to slip objecthood altogether. I mean, of course, *aesthetic* objecthood, and to change one way of appearing for another remains in acquiescence in the view that ones essence is ones *appearance.* So some deeper transformation is required, one to which surfaces, lovely or awful, are irrelevant or merely a fact. The canvases of Arakawa are *irrelevantly* beautiful since not really aesthetic objects at all—as though Arakawa were subtly emphasizing the ontological insight that it is not after all necessary to be ugly in order to escape the servitudes of aesthetics. But escape to *what*? This brings me to the hegelian version of the alternative proposed by Plato to the ephemeralization of art.

Duchamp's *Fountain* is, as everyone knows, to all outward appearances a urinal—it *was* a urinal until it became a work of art and acquired such further properties as works of art possess in exess of those possessed by mere real things like urinals (the work is dated 1917, though it would take research into the history of plumbing to determine the date of the urinal, which made it possible for Duchamp to use urinals dated later than *Fountain* when the original was lost: the *work* remains dated 1917). In his own view he chose this particular object for what he hoped was its aesthetic neutrality. Or pretended that that is what he hoped. For urinals have too strong a cultural, not to say a moral, identity quite to allow themselves to be without affect. They are objects, to begin with, highly sexualized through the fact that women are anatomically barred from employing them in their primary function, at least without awkwardness. So they show their arrogant exclusivity through their form. (The fear of equal access to all johns was a major factor, it will be remembered, in the defeat of the ERA.) They are, moreover, given the cultural realities, objects associated with privacy (though less so than stools) and with dirt. But any object which lies at the intersection of sex and secretion is too obviously charged by the moral boundaries it presupposes *simply* to stand as a culturally neutral object picked out just for its aesthetic neutrality. Duchamp was being disingenuous when he asked: "A urinal—who would be interested in that?" It would be like taking the filthiest verb in the language as one's paradigm for teaching conjugation: *possibly* the word's moral energy will go submerged as one ponders it from the perspective of gerunds and pluperfects, but why struggle when there are plenty of innocent words? It is, meanwhile, ingenuous to treat the urinal *merely* as an aesthetic object, rather like the Taj Mahal in its elegant gradiants and dazzling whiteness.

But then what is the conceptual fulcrum of this still controversial work? My view is that it lies in the question it poses, namely why—referring to itself—should this be an artwork when something else exactly *like* this, namely *that*—referring now to the class of unredeemed urinals—are just pieces of industrial plumbing? It took genius to raise the question in this form, since nothing like it had been raised before, though from Plato (sharply) downward the question of what is art had been raised and unimaginatively answered on the basis of the accepted artworld of the time. Duchamp did not merely raise the question What is Art? but rather Why is something a work of art when something exactly like it is *not*? Compare Freud's great question regarding parapraxes, which is not simply Why do we forget? but Why, when we do forget, do we remember *something else* instead? This form of the question opened space for a radically new theory of the mind. And in Duchamp's case the question he raises *as an artwork* has a genuinely philosophical form, and though it could have been raised with any object you chose (and was raised by means of quite nondescript objects)—in contrast with having been capable of being raised *at any time* you chose—for the question was only historically possible when in fact it was raised—it perhaps required something so antecedently resistant to absorbtion into the artworld as a urinal so as to call attention to the fact that it after all was already *in* the artworld.

There is a deep question of what internal evolution in the history of art made Duchamp's *question-object* historically possible if not historically necessary. My view is that it could only come at a time when it no longer could be clear to anyone what art was while perfectly clear that none of the old answers would serve. To paraphrase Kant, it seemed to have an essence without having any particular essence. It is here that Hegel's views come in.

For Hegel, the world in its historical dimension is the dialectical revelation of consciousness to itself. In his curious idiom, the end of history comes when Spirit achieves awareness of its identity as Spirit, not, that is to say, alienated from itself by ignorance of its proper nature, but united *to* itself *through* itself: by recognizing that it is in this one instance of the same substance as its object, since consciousness of consciousness is consciousness. In the portentous jargon of the

Continent, the subject/object dualism is overcome. Quite apart from such reservations as one must justifiably hold regarding this overcoming, let alone the celebration of it as the end of history, it is worth observing that certain stages in this history are specially marked, art being one stage and philosophy another, and it is the historical mission of art to make philosophy possible, after which art will have no historical mission in the great cosmo-historical sweep. Hegel's stupendous philosophical vision of history gets, or almost gets, an astounding confirmation in Duchamp's work, which raises the question of the philosophical nature of art from *within* art, implying that art already is philosophy in a vivid form, and has now discharged its spiritual mission by revealing the philosophical essence at its heart. The task may now be handed over to philosophy proper, which is equipped to cope with its own nature directly and definitively. So what art finally will have achieved as its fulfillment and fruition is the philosophy of art.

But this is a cosmic way of achieving the second stage of the platonic program, which has always been to substitute philosophy for art. And to dignify art, patronizingly, as philosophy in one of its self-alienated forms, thirsting for clarity as to its own nature as all of us thirst for clarity as to our own. Perhaps there is something to this. When art internalizes its own history, when it becomes self-conscious of its history as it has come to be in our time, so that its consciousness of its history forms part of its nature, it is perhaps unavoidable that it should turn into philosophy at last. And when it does so, well, in an important sense, art comes to an end.

I cannot trace in this essay the structure of such a possible history (but see *"The End of Art"*). My main concern has been to put into perspective the somewhat shabby history of the philosophy of art as a massive political effort either to emasculate or to supersede art. And to sketch certain of the strategies in this long unedifying career. It is always a question in psychotherapy whether the knowledge of the history of a symptom will constitute a cure or merely a kind of acquiescence. Our pathologies may after all, as Freud perhaps realistically affirmed, be the *Kern unser Wesens,* and in the present case art may by now have been so penetrated by its philosophy that we cannot sunder the two in order to rescue art from the conflicts aesthetics has trapped it in.

But in revenge, philosophy has itself become entrapped in its own strategems. If art makes nothing happen and art is but a disguised form of philosophy, philosophy makes nothing happen either. Of course this was Hegel's view. "When philosophy paints its grey in grey," he wrote in one of the most melancholy phrases a philosopher might read, "then has a form of life grown old." Philosophy makes its appearance just when it is too late for anything *but* understanding. So if, according to a ringing slogan, since hardened into a radical cliché of marxism, we want to change rather than understand the world, philosophy cannot be of use. When, then, self-consciousness comes to history, it is by definition too late for something to be made in consequence to happen. So the philosophy of historical being which holds art to be a transform of philosophy shows philosophy to be a transform of art, and this is the great irony of Hegel's theory: the second part of the platonic attack reduces to the first part of the platonic attack, and philosophy, having set itself against art, sets itself finally against itself. This would give us a kind of explanation of the fact that the same structure of argument philosophy mounted at the beginning against art should have returned to call the enterprise of philosophy into question in our own time. So there is an incentive in philosophically curing art of philosophy: we by just that procedure cure philosophy of a paralysis it began its long history by infecting its great enemy with.

Perhaps, for the moment, this is enough by way of speculative philosophy of history. Still, it would be unseemly not to press a bit further, for if neither of the philosophical reasons for pretending that art can make nothing happen is compelling, the fact remains that the history of art is the history of censorship, and it would be interesting to inquire what sort of thing it is that art can make happen, which is of a kind to be regarded dangerous enough to merit, if not suppression then political control. So I will try to end on a somewhat positive note regarding the powers of art.

The first observation to make, admittedly a quite unexciting one, is that once we have separated art from the philosophical theories that have given it its character, the question of whether art makes anything happen is not any longer a philosophically very interesting question. It is, rather, a fairly empirical question, a matter for history or psychology or some social science or other to determine. There are theories of history, marxism being a good example, in which art is excluded from the deep determinants of historical change, since it merely reflects or expresses such changes: it belongs in the superstructure rather than the base of a historical process which moves on two levels, only one of which is effective. Philosophy too has at times been placed in the passive superstructural position by marxists, a self-neutralizing transposition if marxism itself is philosophy and means to change the world: a dilemma neatly sidestepped by marxists treating marxism as a science, and as in the famous linguistics controversy in the Soviet Union, placing science in the dynamic base. A deeper incoherence, it seems to me, is to be found in the repression of certain forms of art, which is after all a benchmark of communist governments which happen also to subscribe to the tenets of Historical Materialism: for if the latter were true, art would be impotent to do anything but express the deep structure of historical reality whatever its form: so repression should be either unnecessary or impossible. It is, to be sure, open to ideologists to say that what does not conform to theory is not art—but this saves theory by trivialization, and leaves us with the anomaly of something evidently effective enough if not suppressed, which would be art were it not ruled out as such by politboro fiat. A less trivializing response would be to say that the offending art reflects a contaminant substructure, and repression will not be needed when the basis is purified of all contradictions. But *that* leaves the question of why mere reflections of the contaminants should be attacked and repressed, since they will vanish when their material conditions do, and it is the material conditions that ought then to be attacked, rather than their superstructural epiphenomena. This is not the place to analyze marxist theories of history, but even if they are true, what follows from them is only that art is impotent to make anything happen *at the base*: so Auden's thought would have to be modified to say that poetry makes nothing *deep* happen. But neither does anything in the superstructure: so why single art out?

Much the same argumentation applies to all those deep theories of history, fortunately or not no longer much in intellectual fashion. Even politics, on these theories, is ineffective but expressive, and Burkhardt's famous chapter "The State as Work of Art" takes on a special meaning against those views of history and historical style which constituted the atmosphere in which he thought. This view of historical style which asks, for example, that we appreciate Abstract Expressionism as expressing the same deep realities politically expressed by Eisenhower foreign policy, McCarthy domestic policy, and the feminine mystique—or Pop Art as expressing the same reality as the politics of Nixon, the Counter-Culture, and the women's liberation movements—tends to dissolve all horizontal relationships between surface phenomena in favor of vertical relationships between surface and depth—with again the consequence that art is not especially more ineffective than anything else on the surfaces of historical change. It requires a very deep view indeed of history to say that politics makes nothing happen. But once we sanely cede power to politics, it becomes difficult to know where the line is to be drawn, and why art should in the end be uniquely ineffectual and merely reflective.

Once we return to surface history—or once we return

surface history to historical effectiveness—it seems simply a matter of fact whether poetry makes anything happen. It would be futile to suppose that poetry readings should have saved the Jews. There are times when the sword is mightier than the pen. But it would only have been against some current of extravagant and immoderate expectations that one could have believed that poetry should have saved the Jews or that folksongs should have saved the whales. Hamlet, for example, believed art could be effective in his own war with Claudius, and he was right, in a way. He was right, however, not because the play within the play was art, but that as art, it was able to communicate as Hamlet perhaps lacked the courage to communicate directly, that Claudius's crime was known to a consciousness other than Claudius's: for how was Claudius otherwise to explain the choice of a drama in any terms other than that Hamlet knew, and meant for Claudius to know that he knew, the bloody truth, and that he had chosen *The Murder of Gonzago* with the intention of conveying this fact? So the play was, metaphorically, a mirror for Claudius, but not for anyone else in the audience, save irrelevantly: and yet it was as much art to them for whom it was not a mirror as to him for whom it was. They were shocked or bored or even amused, and as a general theory of art and its efficacy, Hamlet's theory is a bad one. It is bad as would be a theory that poetry is code when in fact someone writes an anagrammatic poem by means of which the instructed reader can get the formula of the atomic bomb: the little melody in *The Lady Vanishes* encodes some important secret, but its being a folksong has nothing to do with the special uses it might have been put to.

Perhaps what it is unexciting to observe is all there is to observe, though the example just canvassed has the danger of suggesting that art makes something happen only adventitiously, when it is put to an extra-artistic use: and that leaves the familiar thought that intrinsically it makes nothing happen as art. And we are back in the first form of the platonic attack. There must be something wrong with this if I have been at all right in my arguments of *The Transfiguration of the Commonplace* that the structure of artworks is of a piece with the structure of rhetoric, and that it is the office of rhetoric to modify the minds and then the actions of men and women by co-opting their feelings. There are feelings and feelings, on the other hand, some issuing in one kind of action and some in another, and poetry may make something happen if it is successful in promoting action of a sort that may make something happen. And it cannot be extrinsic to the artwork that it should do this if indeed the structure of the work of art and the structure of rhetoric are of a piece. So there is reason after all to be afraid of art.

I am not sure that the structure of rhetoric and the structure of *philosophy* are of a piece, since it is the aim of philosophy to prove rather than merely persuade: but the common structures of rhetoric and art go some distance toward explaining why Plato might have taken a common posture of hostility toward them both and why aesthetic socratism should have seemed so congenial an option. And who knows but that the analogy between artworks and females is due to a reduction of the latter to *feeling* in contrast with reason presumed to be masculine? So that Plato's program of making women the same as men is another aspect of his program of making art the same as philosophy? In any case it has been a long and fateful disenfranchisement, and it will be a task of the following pages to disassemble portions of the philosophy of art from art: all the more timely since there has been a recent effort to deconstruct philosophy by treating it as though it were art!

II.

The Appreciation and Interpretation of Works of Art

*This essay was written for a conference on relativity in the arts, orga-
nized by Betty Jeanne Craige, and held at the University of Georgia in
1982. These auspices explain the few references to relativity in the piece,
which really argues against the premisses of relativism. My view, historically, is that interpretations are discovered and that interpretative statements are true or false. My view, philosophically, is that interpretations
constitute works of art, so that you do not, as it were, have the artwork
on one side and the interpretation on the other. My commentator, Hay-
den White, helped me to see that I was somewhat obscure on this point,
and I hope the present version liquidates that objection. There is a certain overlap to be explained between this essay and chapter 4 of* The
Transfiguration of the Commonplace. *That is because only after that
book went to press did I discover what I really ought to have said. This is
the one place where the argument of that book is superseded rather than
merely amplified and extended. The essay first appeared in* Relativism
in the Arts, *edited by Professor Craige, and published by the University
of Georgia Press.*

GENIUS, ACCORDING TO Schopenhauer, is the capacity for
knowing the Ideas of things—in the platonic sense of Ideas—
and for revealing these Ideas in works of art for the benefit of

the remainder of mankind who, borrowing as it were the eyes of genius, may behold through these works what the genius beholds directly. "The work of art is only a means for facilitating this knowledge," Schopenhauer writes, treating art as a cognitive prosthetic, a metaphysical window through which we may view the deeper realities, but which in no further sense has any cognitive contribution of its own to make at all: it is to be seen through, but not itself to be seen—so the more transparent the better. Aesthetic response, accordingly, is not to be elicited directly by the work of art as such, which aspires to a kind of nothingness, but rather by what the work of art discloses or, as the aestheticians of the eighteenth century would have said, *discovers* or, since we are being historical, as Heidegger would say, *unconceals*. As the work of art is really only what it is of, Schopenhauer feels justified in saying that "aesthetic pleasure is one and the same, whether called for by a work of art or directly by the contemplation of life and nature."

The ideal of the self-diaphanizing artwork is very ancient. It is, for example, a fantasy of the mimetic theory of art that the work of art should present to eye or ear only what would have been presented them by the object imitated. As such, presentation underdetermines the distinction between reality and art, to which it is invariant, and illusion becomes not only a possibility but a goal. The gauzy essence of art is perhaps enshrined in the wider concept of the *medium*, as that which sacrifices its own identity that an Other should be made present through it, whether in the spiritualistic parlor where the departed soul communicates through the medium, gone symbolically unconscious; or in the concert hall, where the performer acts as a kind of medium through which the music is made audible (a pianist of obviously extraordinary gifts was recently disqualified from the Chopin competition on the grounds that his flashy playing occluded the music it was his task to make present); or on the theatrical stage where the highest art of acting is no evident acting at all, as when the audience becomes conscious not of

Proust's Berma, but instead of Phèdre herself, to the end of whose enfleshment Berma had the uncanny knack of disappearing as herself (in his autobiography the British actor Alec McGowen recalls having gotten too many laughs in his role as Hadrian VII, concluding that it was the performance rather than the role, contrary to the requirements of serious comedy, that amused his audience).

Art, on this view, aims exactly at the sort of nothingness Sartre supposes consciousness to exemplify, as it is ontologically disqualified to be an object, at least for itself; or which Berkeley speaks of as spirituality, in the respect that spirits are never present to themselves as their ideas are—can form no idea of themselves—because they instead are the media through which ideas are given. Since not an object unless it falls short of its intentions, the fact that it is an artwork is to play no role of its own in provoking aesthetic responses, which are only to what the medium contains—the "content"—and which are the same whether the content is confronted directly, as by Schopenhauer's genius, or as a *pis allé* through a glass clearly.

It is possible to appreciate the recent history of art as a philosophical effort to reassert its own identity, to infuse with itself the space theory had required it to vacate, to clot that emptiness and spurn the thin rewards of mediumhood by drawing attention to itself, sometimes brashly: to become "a reality," as artists are fond of saying. And one stratagem for achieving this has been more or less to turn the tables on reality by forcing undeniably real objects to serve as media, possessing them like spooks, so that the works of such masters of reverse artistic magic as Marcel Duchamp present themselves in the bodies of objects we would have no way of knowing were not snow shovels or bottle racks, bicycle wheels or grooming combs. But perfect embodiment, like perfect transparency, seems ironically to leave the work of art as weightless as ever: for what have we here to respond to save the snow shovel itself, however possessed? And Schopenhauer's contention that aesthetic pleasure is one and

the same appears to have an even greater claim to consideration, for artwork and crass object are as indiscernible as
two crass objects of the same unedifying type. It is comical
how little difference it seems to make whether art is an airy
nothing revealing reality in its nakedness, or so gluts itself
with reality that between reality and itself there is no visible
difference.

So imagine three altogether similar snow shovels, all
from the same factory, one of which is definitely a work of
art, though not to be told apart from its vastly less illustrious
peers by protracted and minute inspection, not least of all
because, though an artwork, it remains also what it has been
all along, an outdoor tool of seasonal use. The question of
the nature of art arises with this "also," for what apart from
and in addition to its identity as a snow shovel does it "also"
have which makes of it an ontological companion of
L'embarquement à Cythère or *Tristan und Isolde*? And can the
fact that it is an artwork ("also") make any aesthetic difference? If aesthetic response is always and only to what meets
the eye (or ear or whatever other sense), it is difficult to see
where aesthetic difference can lie, given the indiscrim-
inability of our snow shovels. So if there is to be a difference,
it must lie logically hidden from the senses in what remains
over when we subtract snow shovel from artwork—which is
like seeking for the soul by subtracting the body from the
person when it is not clear that there *is* a remainder. And in
the case of works of art it is difficult to see what aesthetic
response could amount to if it is to be to something so singularly impalpable.

I nevertheless wish to argue that Schopenhauer is
wrong, and that the fact that something is an artwork makes
an aesthetic difference, even if the artwork it is is not to be
told apart from a mere thing like a snow shovel. And this
means that the work of art cannot be identified either with
the *néant* of mimetic evanescence nor the *être* of duchampian
achievement: Being and Nothingness cannot exhaust the
metaphysical plane if works of art are to have a locus on it.

Aesthetically speaking, the two comically interlocked theories of art are equivalent. So I shall use the possibility of aesthetic difference to prepare the stage, which has been dominated by comedians who merely interchange masks, for another sort of theory altogether.

That another sort of theory altogether is required may be gathered from the fact that both the theories just caricatured give us the same thing as subject for aesthetic predicates, and neither can in consequence be adequate to what we may term the language of the art world. That this has not until now been gathered may be explained by the fact that it has been the concept of beauty which has dominated aesthetic discussion down the ages, a fixation which has blinded philosophers to the richness of this language and concealed from them its logic. The Transparency theory of art withdraws from aesthetic consideration, of course, everything except the content of the work, the rest being excrescence not bearing on the essence of art. The Reality theory withdraws from art everything except the reality which would be the content of the artwork as construed by the Transparency theory. So whatever aesthetic predicates apply, apply to that invariant thing, whatever it may be. To be sure, it would hardly have occurred to the artists of Schopenhauer's time to have revealed an Idea so contaminated with *Alltäglichkeit* as a snow shovel, the lessons of caravaggism not having been thought through to their limit. So let us take some flowers. Aesthetically speaking, it little matters whether it is a diaphanized representation of flowers, or a bunch of flowers elevated by the Flower Artist, who uses daffodils as her material, into a work of art, or *just* a bunch of flowers. Aesthetically, the differences are inscrutable. A beautiful representation of flowers is just a representation of beautiful flowers, as the Transparency theory gives us nothing but the content of the work to serve as subject for aesthetic predication. And the flowers, let us grant, are beautiful, whether those taken up into the artworld by the Flower Artist using the zero degree of artistic intervention, or those, otherwise exactly like them, she happens not to have left deliberately untouched. These were touched by my friend and neighbor Ellen Williams, a very nice woman but not an artist, and certainly not the Flower Artist. They are beautiful in their sameness, irrespective of ontology.

The Transparency theory gives a formula for creating beautiful works of art, namely "Pick a beautiful object and represent it with maximum transparency." Such was the formula of the ancient Greeks, as Lessing characterizes them in Laocoön: "The wise Greek confined painting strictly to the imitation of beauty: the Greek artist imitated nothing that was not beautiful." The Reality theory abbreviates the creative procedures radically, its formula being: pick a beautiful object and let it be a work of art. The aesthetic theory in either case is this: if the subject of the work is F, for any aesthetic predicate F, the work will be F if suitably transparent. And here precisely is the trouble with the concept of beauty. Things in the world, say flowers, can be beautiful in ways which do not make puzzling, much less conspicuously nonsensical, the inference from beautiful paintings of x's to paintings of beautiful x's. The moment we avert our eyes from beauty and survey the wider resources of our aesthetic vocabulary, however, we may begin to have doubts about this inference even in the case of beauty. I am thinking just now of some powerful drawings of flowers I would resist describing as drawings of powerful flowers. I would resist it because I am uncertain whether there are any powerful flowers, and because I am certain that if there are any, these snapdragons and irises are not. Yet "powerful" is a commonplace item in the language of the artworld. But in fact there is scarcely a predicate of ordinary discourse which cannot be pressed into aesthetic service. So there are fluid drawings and clunky drawings, fragile drawings and witty drawings, explosive drawings and childlike drawings of flowers which even in the most likely case are probably not fragile by anything like the same criteria drawings of them are. It is not my intention in this essay to elaborate the logic of these predicates, or their psychology, but only to say that there has to be some subject for them which neither of the theories considered can identify, and to draw out a few philosophical lessons before proceeding to my main preoccupations.

First of all, so long as philosophical attention was fixated on the concept of beauty, it was possible to speculate that there might be a *sense* of beauty, through the avenue of which the aesthetical qualities of things would be conveyed to consciousness—as we become conscious of the colors of things through the visual sense. From the sensibility theorists of the Enlightenment to the bloomsbury intuitionists, the idea that aesthetic appreciation presupposed some sort of *Anschauung* was allowed by the concept of beauty to be more or less taken for granted. But there could hardly be a temptation to postulate a special sense for each of the aesthetic predicates—a sense of powerfulness, or fragility, or clunkiness. Moral vocabulary is also rich and varied, but it was possible to suppose that goodness entered into the definition of every such predicate, and that goodness itself was, as it were, intuited by a special moral sense. It is unlikely that a parallel theory is available for beauty, and in general it seems to me that one consequence of merely just noting the extensiveness of the aesthetic vocabulary is to dim the attractiveness of the sensation model for aesthetic understanding. Indeed, aesthetic understanding of works of art may be far closer to an intellectual action than a mode of sensory stimulation or passion, at least when dealing with works of art.

Second, it is perhaps unclear whether the sorts of aesthetic predicates I am referring to apply under the same criteria to works of art and to mere real things when the latter are addressed aesthetically. It is a fact about flowers that they are fragile, and their fragility, which is factual, has made flowers natural metaphors for fading insubstantialities elsewhere in the world: for physical beauty, innocence, virtue, youth, and happiness. Cherry blossoms in Japan occasion thoughts of

the fleetingness of life: but then we are viewing these show-
ers of pink and white petals under the framework afforded
by a kind of philosophy of life and treating them virtually
from the perspectives of art. Abstracted from these metaphorical and philosophical impulses, would the fragility of
flowers ever become a matter of aesthetic focus? Enjoined to
heed the fragility of flowers, I take this either as an injunc-
tion to watch my clumsy step or to see them as the subject of
a poem. Ernest Gombrich's clever remark that we *see* what
we paint is not, really, a thesis about optics, but of the manner in which the theories about life and the world affect the
way we respond to the world. So when someone says, as
Marx Wartofky has done, that El Greco has enabled him to
see the elongatedness of things, treating Greco as an optical
revelator, he is overlooking the possibility that elongation is
the artistic expression of the opposed tension between earth
and heaven Greco's stretched saints metaphorically exhibit.
In fact it is possible to argue that the language of the artworld
is metaphoric in its semantics. True, this may mean that
Schopenhauer's thesis stands, that aesthetic response is the
same whether to artworks or real things, but this will be
because real things are seen under the perspective of art
when responded to aesthetically. So we can save the thesis
only by rotating it through 180 degrees. This, to be sure,
leaves the concept of beauty to be dealt with if this is the one
main concept to which the distinction between nature and
art, at least when art is explained through either of the theories here canvassed, is indifferent. But then we are left with a
curious question of what save the predicates of beauty could
have formed the critical discourse of the ancients, and it
leaves us with the thought that their experience of art must
have been singularly impoverished relative to our own if all
they could say was, "How beautiful!" To be sure, they could
also praise artworks for their transparency—viz., the grapes
he painted looked good enough to eat, the woman he carved
looked soft enough to love, etc.

Finally we may note the irrelevance of aesthetic considerations to the deep problems of the philosophy of art, which have to do with answering the question our trio of snow shovels raises, namely to distinguish the one that is art from the one that is not. If Schopenhauer is right, the aesthetic qualities are of a piece as between art and reality, and we hardly can distinguish things on the basis of what they have in common. If he is wrong, then the fact that something is an artwork makes an aesthetic difference. But then the aesthetic difference presupposes the distinction we are after and cannot be part of what makes that difference. So aesthetics does not pertain to the essence of art—which does not mean that we won't learn something about aesthetics from identifying that essence. So back to our snow shovels.

The snow shovel which "also" is an artwork suitably bears a title, in this instance "In Advance of The Broken Arm," at first glance one of Duchamp's lamer jokes. But then one comes to see that no one is going to break his (or her?) arm shoveling snow with "In Advance of the Broken Arm" just because its promotion to the status of art lifts it above, or at any rate outside the domain of the mere utensil, and so there is a tension after all between work of art and tool which the title wittily underlines. An important subgenre of Duchamp's *oeuvre* may be appreciated as so many wry comments on the witty thesis of Kant's, according to which art is to be viewed in terms of a generalized purposefulness which yet cannot be identified with any specific purpose, as though the question of what its use is is always legitimate though no answer is allowed as correct. Duchamp shows us tools stripped of their usefulness by their uncomfortable new status, *Zuhandene* thrust into the domain of *Vorhandene*, to use Heidegger's political metaphor, as out of place as a plumber at an April in Paris ball. Duchamp makes the metaphysical homelessness of these objects vivid and even intoxicating— but then, surely, appreciation of these works must in part consist in feeling the philosophical tensions they must give rise to, rather than, as it were, mooning over their Significant Forms or whatever. It would be an ironic and irrelevant fact, for instance, if the ratio of diameter to height in Warhol's Campbell Soup Can happened exactly to satisfy the Golden Section!

　　Consider in this respect Duchamp's celebrated work, so often referred to in these essays, *Fountain,* of 1917, which as every one knows was but a urinal of that period disconnected from the plumbing which gives it its familiar utility—familiar at least to just under half the population of the West—and turned on its back like an immobilized turtle. It is a piece of industrial porcelain, purchased by Duchamp (himself!) from among its undistinguished lookalikes produced by a company called Mott Works. It is inconsistent with the spirit of the work to imagine Duchamp anxiously examining the urinals in the salesplace until he found "just the right one." Indeed, the original has been lost (it exists only in a famous photograph taken by Alfred Stieglitz), but Duchamp purchased another one for the Sidney Janis Gallery and a third for the Galleria Schwartz in Milan, and in fact subsequently put out an edition of eight, signed and numbered, as though he had issued an edition of etchings. The signature is Duchamp's, though the name—"R. Mutt"—is not, though as we know, Duchamp gave himself various names for various other subgenres of his output—e.g., "Rrose Selavy" for his erotica, etc. The difference between name and signature may have struck the artworld of his time as odder than it would today, when one of the main loci of graffiti, aside from subway cars, are men's rooms; and it is a convention of this form of art that its executants conceal their identity under special *noms de crayon,* splashed on in manner no less than in form that little distinguishes "R. Mutt 1917" from "Taki 191" or "Zorbo 219," save the extra digit. Its being a signature, of course, goes with its being a work of art, a status acknowledged by the Hanging Committee of the Independents Exhibition of 1917 who *rejected* it—you don't reject *things* from art shows, you exclude them. Of course the designer of that urinal, proud of his work, might have signed it—artisans, after all, also sign their productions, as collectors of antiques know, but the crudeness with which "R. Mutt 1917" is splashed on is inconsistent with pride of artisanship. It is a perfectly elegant bit of ceramics, but its elegance is scarcely relevant to appreciating the artwork, of which the signature, which cannot here be separated from the work, is as inelegant as it can be. So it should be plain that Duchamp was not redeeming for aesthetic delectation an object up to then deemed crass beyond consideration, a reminder, say, that beauty is to be found in the least likely places. But the grip of aestheticism on the philosophy of art is strong and cold, as may be gathered from the fact that the aesthetic qualities of the urinal are taken to be what *Fountain* is all about in the view of George Dickie, the institutionalist theoretician of art, who partially defines art in terms of its candidacy for appreciation. And exactly aesthetic appreciation must be meant if his defense of this theory is to make sense. "Why ," Dickie asks, "cannot the ordinary qualities of *Fountain*—its gleaming white surface, the depth revealed when it reflects images or surrounding objects, its pleasing oval shape—be appreciated? It has qualities similar to those of works by Brancusi and Moore, which many do not balk at saying they appreciate." These *are* qualities of the urinal in question, as they are qualities of all those heavy-duty numbers from Mott Works in that era. And these *are* qualities in part shared by that part of Brancusi's *Bird in Flight* which itself was classed as an industrial product by a sensitive customs inspector. As a matter of art-historical fact, we know that Duchamp seized upon his readymades precisely because they were in his view aesthetically indifferent. One of these, a metal comb with the dumb title "Comb"—or perhaps not so dumb, since the literal reading of it would cause us to overlook a neatly inscribed nonsense phrase (*Trois ou quatre gouttes de hauteur n'ont rien a voir avec la sauvagerie*) along its spine—possesses what Duchamp identifies as "the characteristics of the true readymade":

During the 48 years since it was chosen as a readymade this little
iron comb has kept the characteristics of the true readymade: No
beauty, no ugliness, nothing particularly aesthetic about it . . . it
was not even stolen in all those 48 years!

Professor Ted Cohen has claimed that the work is not the
urinal at all, but the gesture of exhibiting it: and gestures are
of just the wrong type to have surfaces, gleaming or dull.
Cohen thus locates *Fountain* in the genre of the happening
rather than, as would be my inclination, as a contribution to
the history of sculpture. To be sure, an argument is available
that sculptors can shape events as well as matter, and function in time as well as in space. But the existence of dupli-
cates and replicae goes counter to this classification—it is not
the gesture of exhibition which is duplicated but the urinal
together with whatever makes it art—and moreover the gesture of exhibition, which is witty and daring and brash, is not
in the spirit of the readymade, which is supposed to be dull.
So the work is rather more conservative than Cohen supposes. That such a theory as Cohen's is available at all, however, is evidence that the identity of the work is pretty indeterminate even at present writing, and, as different aesthetic
qualities go with the various interpretations—Dickie's white
radiance, Cohen's audacity—it is difficult to know what to
appreciate until we know how the work is to be interpreted.

The anonymous defender of *Fountain* in the second issue
of the fly-by-night journal *The Blind Man*—not coinciden-
tally published by Duchamp himself, among others—writes
thus: "Mr. Mutt . . . took an ordinary article of life, placed it
so that its useful significance disappeared under the new title
and point of view—created a new thought for that object."
The "thought" must concern the power of titles to exsub-
stantiate objects as resistant to sublation as urinals must be,
considering that it is the urinal which remains the object of
critical consciousness to this very day, and so it is not clear
that the power in question extends quite that far. What we
have is the giddy spectacle of a concept—the concept of art—
which has bitten off more than it can chew, like a hapless

python with an unswallowable lump in its suddenly inadequate gullet. It could be a metaphor for the ultimate resistance of art to being ingested by its own philosophy. In
any case, what "Mr. Mutt" is claimed to have created is a *new*
thought for *that* object: so that work must be thought *cum*
object, taken together, and the object, accordingly, is only
part of the work. So the object may indeed have those
qualities singled out by Dickie, without it following that the
work must have them: and so appreciation remains in sus-
pense, pending the outcome of interpreting.

Fountain is not to every artlover's taste, and I confess that
much as I admire it philosophically, I should, were it given
me, exchange it as quickly as I could for more or less than
any Chardin or Morandi—or even, given the exaggerations
of the art market, for a middling chateau in the valley of the
Loire. But this has nothing to do with my taste for glistering
white porcelain, which I greatly prefer to the decorator colors found in middle-class johns across the continent, as being somehow more "classic." But for just these reasons I
find, and think anyone sharing my tastes would find, something repulsive in the smeary "R. Mutt 1917," which would
send me pretty quickly to the Ajax can and Brillo box. Taste,
after all, has its consistencies, even if it is relative and the
paradigm of what cannot be rationally disputed. So let us
ponder the inadvertent vandalism of someone who scours
off that hideous lettering, thinking it is graffiti, in order to
stand back and vibrate to the arctic sublimities of Mott
Works's finest, responding aesthetically to an object pure in
curvature and colorlessness, a bare bit of beauty fit for Eu-
clid's cold eye, perhaps a joy forever. Under so exalted a perspective, it ought not to matter where or when the object was
made, or even that it *was* made by human intervention, for
it is possible to imagine the right combination of kaolin,
feldspar, and quartz, shaped and fired in the bowels of the
earth at 700 to 800 degrees F, and discovered by Bouvard

and Pecuchet, who donate it to the Natural History Museum while its counterpart, this time by virtue of a historical rather than a geological counterfactual, lies across the Marie-Theresien-Platz, where it was brought as artistic booty by the victorious Austro-Hungarians in 1918, and placed in the *Kunsthistorische Museum* next to the Breugels. What an inspired curatorial choice, considering that Flemish master's well-known penchant for urinary wit!

Purity of response goes with purity of object, which means, I suppose, the object purified of any historical or cultural associations. So the muttless object could have any number of histories, for all our aestheticism decrees. Alas, Vienna lacks an oriental museum, but we can perhaps imagine Prince Eugene of Savoy prevailed upon to build one in order to house one of the prizes. The Chinese were the finest ceramicists known, and I can imagine them having produced circa A.D. 1000 an object just like ours, made deliberately perforated to render it conspicuously useless for the residual purposes of Chinese porcelain, whose paradigmatic exemplars would be jars and pots, in order to emphasize that *this* was intended *only* for contemplation by those responsive to the white mists and waterfalls of the Sung, and to emblemize the Neo-confucian teaching that works of art are to be treated as ends withal, and never as means. What I mean to say is that it is easy to fit the identical object—identical at least under one-place predicates, whether these have primary, secondary, or, as some aestheticians suppose, tertiary properties as their extensions—into different contexts, in each of which we in fact, if the object is in that context an artwork as it is in two of those just laid out, respond to something which is not presented to the senses, not even augmented by the sense of beauty. But let us suppose that lesson understood, and focus for analytical purposes on those properties which do present themselves to the senses, and on some of which the eye (for instance) may dwell just for the pleasure it derives from what it dwells on.

Suppose there are choices made for purely aesthetic reasons, where by "purely aesthetic reasons" I mean that these are choices of what we *simply* prefer, without having been taught to prefer it, and without further reasons for preference. Kepler, had he had his way with the universe, would have preferred circular to elliptical orbits for his planets, but this because he had internalized a set of metaphysical reasons which mandated circular motion as somehow the most *perfect* sort of motion: ellipses seemed unworthy of a universe designed by a Perfect Being. The physicist Rainwater won the Nobel Prize for his suggestion that certain puzzling properties of the nucleus would follow as a matter of course if the nucleus were shaped like a cigar, an ignominious form because of whose ignominy Rainwater's conjecture met resistance, since scientists were convinced, for who knows what deep reasons—and this in 1958!—that the nucleus had to be a *sphere*. As with shapes, so with colors. White is a metaphor for purity and "because of its purity" is a reason for preferring white to scarlet, which connects the choice to background imperatives in the religious unconscious. Scarlet is the hue of sin, if we suppress the thought of cardinal robes, doubtless because it is the color of fire, and fire is, for reasons which if not obvious will never be found out, a metaphor for anger and sexual passion. And so on. But there are choices made by animals at the operant level which have to be explained aesthetically, without their aesthetics being explained by their beliefs: there are things which dogs and cats like, smells and tastes, just because they do like them. There may be causes in the DNA material, without the animal having reasons. These would then be pure aesthetic choices. I expect we make them too.

Writing on the topic of boredom, with which some of his work is associated, Warhol says that it is important to sit and watch the same thing—"I don't want it to be essentially the same, I want it to be exactly the same. Because the more you look at the same exact thing, the more the meaning goes away and the better and emptier you feel." This sounds about like a formula for contemplation, where any suffi-

ciently dull object—a door knob, one's own navel—is a
means for attaining that good empty feeling Warhol's fellow
mystics tend to pursue. But I wish to stress the disappearance of meaning, leaving the bare object, even if, living
as we do in intensionalized, situationalized worlds, it is far
from plain, as I sought to argue above, that very much aesthetically will remain when meaning is subtracted. In any
case it would only be under such subtraction that the object
which remains would give rise in us to what I am calling *pure*
aesthetic responses. Now taste, as a matter of conceptual
truth, is relative, even if in fact every one always prefers the
same thing, and so suppose that it is established by psychol-
ogists and anthropologists, working as they do with neonates, exotic tribes, total amnesiacs, hydrocephalics, that
there is a universal spontaneous aesthetic preference for just
the object Duchamp happens to have chosen for *Fountain*,
invariantly as to questions of meaning and background metaphysics: that he has discovered the Universal Aesthetic Object! After all, there has to be some reason why the designer
at Mott Works chose that modified trifoil over the countless
forms available to much the same function. All this is meant
to get us as close to an aesthetic *tabula rasa* as can be imagined, and the only purpose for doing this is to show that
nothing remotely like this is available for *Fountain* itself, as
an artwork, whatever delight the object it is materially related to may bring to the uncontaminated seventh sense of
newborn babes and Bushmen. It would indeed not be possible to run the experiment with neonates under Fountain's
identity as a work of art. For while they may have an overwhelming, irresistible propensity for contemplating *that object*, they are conceptually innocent of what an artwork is.
There is something to which the neonate is blind that the
critic of *Blind Man* could see—namely that, whatever it is,
which is not merely adjoined to the seductive form of world-
wide charm, but may in fact cause that form to go under: to
"disappear." It is not even clear what color *Fountain* is, or if it
has a color. It is to this rather than what we can nakedly

aestheticize that we must look to see what an artwork is.
And a very different sort of aesthetic than pure aesthetic
responses exemplify will be called for.

It will have been observed that indiscernible objects become, quite different and distinct works of art by dint of
distinct and different interpretations, so I shall think of interpretations as functions which transform material objects into
works of art. Interpretation is in effect the lever with which
an object is lifted out of the real world and into the artworld, where it becomes vested in often unexpected raiment.
Only in relationship to an interpretation is a material object
an artwork, which of course does not entail that what is
an artwork is relative in any further interesting way. The
artwork a thing becomes may have in fact a remarkable
stability.

Not every artwork, it perhaps goes without saying, is a
transform through an interpretation of an *objet trouvé,* and
with most works of art it takes some trouble to imagine
counterparts to them, as with our triad of snow shovels,
which are not works of art, chiefly because most artworks
are objects thrust into the world with the intention that they
be works of art. Still, as I hope I have shown, here as elsewhere, it is always possible, for any artwork you choose, to
imagine something indiscernible from it but caused in a way
which renders a transformative interpretation inapplicable.
Which does not mean that the object is beyond redemption—it can be interpreted into arthood—but it scarcely
could be the work we have in mind in imagining this new
but perfectly congruent thing. Suppose, as a cultural ter-
rorist, I decide to blow up the marble quarries at Carrara, to
make a statement once and for all of the politico-moral cor-
ruption of the Renaissance. I plant tons of plastic explosive
and depress the detonator with a song of anarchy on my lips.
The dust clears, and there in the midst of it all, the lumps of
marble have fallen together to form what could not be told

apart from the *Tempietto* of Bramante—except for the fact that
it is topped by what cannot be told apart from the *Pietà with
St. Nicodemus* of Michelangelo. That sculpture would be radically out of place atop that exquisite structure, an adorable
architectural metaphor whereby a roman templum is transfigured into an emblem of Roman Christianity, and historical
continuity as well as religious triumph is celebrated through
monumental reference. But this curiously shaped hunk of
marble is no more out of place atop this pile of marble lumps
than anything else would be. Or rather: there is no room
here for the concept of place: we have only a statistically odd
jumble of rock, fallen where it has fallen and as it has fallen,
and, external similarities notwithstanding, there is nothing
here of reference or metaphor. Not that jumbles cannot be
metaphors, only this isn't. Of course it could be a miracle, a
benign bit of meddling on the part of the spirit of Pope Julius
II: but even so it could not mean what the *Tempietto* of Bramante means, even if *I* convert on the spot. So though an
artist might have planted all that plastic and detonated it in
the hope that something *just like this* would happen, I am
uncertain what work he has produced and seek for interpretation: but it won't be the interpretation which gives the
Tempietto its locus in the history of Renaissance architecture.
But enough.

There are two sorts of mistakes the concept of art gives
rise to, one of which is philosophical and the other merely
critical. The first is to interpret something which is not in
candidacy for art, and the second consists in giving the
wrong interpretation of the right sort of thing. I may go
through the motions of interpreting the snow shovel when I
discover that I have interpreted the wrong one, which is different from discovering that I have given the wrong interpretation of the proper object. There are views of artistic
interpretation in which, while it may be correct or incorrect
to interpret a given object, there is no correct or incorrect
interpretation. You have yours and I have mine. I would like
to spend the remainder of this essay in exploring enough of

the logic of artistic interpretation to imply a view on this extreme sort of relativism.

The Fourteenth Edition of the *Encyclopaedia Britannica* defines *fountain* as an arrangement for letting water gush into an ornamental basin, as well as, one may suppose through metonymy, the ornamental receptacle or "the jet of water itself." Mott Works's urinal fits this definition pretty perfectly, which, had Duchamp been bent on lexicographical mischief, would have put the definers to some labor to exclude this unwelcome newcomer to the range of the definiendum because of slackness in the definiens. I think his intentions were less to get urinals classed as fountains, which would make his title into a label, than, leaving its connotations intact, as a civilized device for relief of cystic distension, and thrusting it metaphorically under the attributes of fountains as works of sculptural architecture, compassing such achievements as the Schöner Brunnen of Nuremberg, the Fontana di Trevi in Rome, the Fontaine des Innocents by Jean Goujon in Paris, Paul Manship's Prometheus Fountain in Rockefeller Plaza, and not least of all the *Mannequin Pisse* of the sculptor Duquesnoy in Brussels, upon which, to show how mores may have changed from 1619 to 1917, Louis XV is said to have conferred the coveted Croix de St. Louis. His identification of this as a fountain is, then, not a classification but an interpretation: saying of that urinal that *it* is a fountain is indeed an instance of what I have elsewhere termed an *artistic identification,* where the "is" in question is consistent (but only consistent) with the literal falsity of the identification. Thus it is artistically true but literally false to say of a certain piece of shaped marble that it is St. Nicodemus, or of a certain young singer that she is the love-hungry young man Cherubino, or of a piece of fictional prose that it is a letter from Pamela. But *Campbell's Soup Can* really is a can of Campbell's soup.

Interpretations pivot on artistic identifications, and these in turn determine which parts and properties of the object in question belong to the work of art into which interpretation transfigures it. So we could as easily characterize interpretations as functions which impose artworks onto material objects, in the sense of determining which properties and parts of the latter are to be taken as part of the work and within the work significant in a way they characteristically are not outside the work. If "R. Mutt 1917" *in fact* were graffiti, it would disfigure the urinal but not necessarily the work, as a blot of spilled ink may damage a book but not in any sense affect the novel, unless the novel itself is a kind of *roman-objet* in the genre of *Tristram Shandy.* And in ruining the book it may destroy something of far greater value than the work, which may be trash. The cracks which appear in the glass panels of Duchamp's *La mariée mise a nu par ses célébataires, même* damaged the object and obscured the work until, leaving the damaged object where it was, Duchamp made them part of the work, enlisting as unwitting collaborator the shoddy freight handler. The object proved fragile, but it is not even remotely clear what would be meant in saying that the *work* is fragile: the aesthetic predicate "fragile" would seem not to apply to this boisterous image of oblique eroticism in which, in Richard Hamilton's words, "The Bride hangs stripped yet inviolate in her glass cage, while the bachelors grind their chocolate below." One may note, by the way, that a copy of the Great Glass would be considerably more difficult to execute than *Le grand verre* itself, despite which two full-scale copies of it were made, the first by Ulf Linde in 1961 and the second by Richard Hamilton even, in 1966, at Newcastle-upon-Tyne. No one wants to take a chance shipping the original about.

I am trying to say that decisions have to be made of a sort which do not arise with mere real things. Even if one tries to cut things short by saying that the work consists in the whole damned thing, there will always remain a problem of where the boundaries of the whole damned thing are. Consider one last time the snow shovels, and let every part of the relevant snow shovel indeed be part of *In Advance of the Broken Arm.* But what about its position? Should it be right-side up or upside-down, on its back or on its front? Does it or does it not make a difference which? Suppose one asks: does it mean anything that *In Advance of the Broken Arm* stands upright? And the answer may be that it does not, because its having this or that position, while a property of the snow shovel, is not really a property of the work. Of an ordinary snow shovel, one again may ask what it means that it is in this position or that, but there can be no shirking at least the appropriateness of the question, for there is always by grace of the principle of sufficient reason an answer: it was left just there and has not been moved, it was knocked over by the dog, it just fell. The principle of sufficient reason also may apply to artworks, but we may be mistaken that there is something in them that requires that sort of explanation. Only what falls under an interpretation is a legitimate ex-planandum.

It has at times given me pleasure to imagine whole gal-leries of artworks from whose descriptions it could not be deduced that the material objects each is connected with look exactly alike: galleries of snow shovels, or squares of red canvas, or paintings only one of which happens to be *The Polish Rider* of Rembrandt. The philosopher Odo Marquart has chided me for extravagance: why not have just one square of red canvas, given the ways of the art market, and decorate the walls with interpretations? I am uncertain the relationship between artwork and material object is quite so casual that the time and place and causes of the object are indifferent to the identity of the work, even though they may differ, as the date of the readymade will differ from the date on which that particular comb has been manufactured. But this is not altogether the problem of concern to me, but rather the fact that the phenomenal indiscernibility of these material objects underdetermines the artworks in question in a way which must remind the sophisticates of those issues of radical translation with which Professor Quine has plagued the philosophy of language in recent times. Even if we knew which objects were up for artistic interpretation, how could we determine which interpretation is correct? Is *correct:* for not even Quine would wish to say that anything goes. If anything went, the skeptical problems induced by radical translation would disappear, as there is the possibility of being wrong only if there is the possibility of being right. And the fact that there can be imagined countless works which all look alike does not mean that of the same object countless interpretations can be given if the object is in candidacy to begin with. Modern critical theory appears to subscribe to a theory of endless interpretation, almost as though the work were after all a kind of mirror in which each of us sees something different (ourselves), and where the question of the *correct* mirror image can make no sense. I shall suppose that if there is an analogy to Quine's problem, there is meaning to the notion of being wrong, which requires that the question of correctness can arise, and, hence, crudely speaking, interpretation is not endless after all.

I believe we cannot be deeply wrong if we suppose that the correct interpretation of object-as-artwork is the one which coincides most closely with the artist's own interpretation. Coinciding interpretations put us in different posture with regard to artists than undertaking to discover what their intentions may have been, nor is it as a thesis subject to the sorts of objections Susan Sontag raises against interpretation generally. For the interpretations she impugns only begin or can begin when the work of art is in place, established as such, and the interpreter begins to ponder what the artist is "really" doing or what the work "really" means. Hers is against a notion of interpretation which makes the artwork as an explanandum—as a symptom, for example. My theory of interpretation is instead constitutive, for an object is an artwork *at all* only in relation to an interpretation. We may bring this out in a somewhat logical way. Interpretation in my sense is transfigurative. It transforms objects into works of art, and depends upon the "is" of artistic identification. Her interpretations, which are explanatory, use instead the "is" of ordinary identity. Her despised interpreters see works as signs, symptoms, expressions of ulterior or subjacent realities, states of which are what the artwork "really" refers to, and which requires the interpreter to be master of one or another kind of code: psychoanalytical, culturographic, semiotical, or whatever. In effect, her interpreters address the work in the spirit of science, and it may very well be that the endlessness of textual interpretation derives from the endlessness of scientific perspectives under which a work may be viewed. We know too little of man, really, to pretend that no new or fresh insights into art may not open up in the human sciences of the future. In this sense, the artist can scarcely be any more conscious of these interpretations than we. We need not therefore know much about the artist at all when we seek to confirm these interpretations. Sontag then is arguing against *Literaturwissenschaft,* in effect: she is saying, and perhaps is right in saying, that it will not necessarily make literature more available to us nor make us better readers. She is being anti-intellectual and saying: the work gives you everything you need to know about it if what you want is literary experience: pay attention to *it.* With those sorts of interpretations, the artist is certainly in no privileged position.

Mine is a theory which is not in the spirit of science but of philosophy. If interpretations are what constitute works, there are no works without them and works are misconstituted when interpretation is wrong. And knowing the artist's interpretation is in effect identifying what he or she has made. The interpretation is not something outside the work: work and interpretation arise together in aesthetic consciousness. As interpretation is inseparable from work, it is inseparable from the artist if it is the artist's work.

How close is my interpretation in the case of *Fountain* to Duchamp's? Close enough, I suppose, and in any case the work I have sought to constitute *could* be the work he made. The possible interpretations are constrained by the artist's location in the world, by when and where he lived, by what experiences he could have had. An object indiscernible from the one I have been discussing could have come about in many ways at many times and be the work it is. There is a truth to interpretation and a stability to works of art which are not relative at all.

III.

Deep Interpretation

But if you were to hide the world in the
world so that nothing could get away, this
would be the final reality of the constancy
of things.
　　—Chuang Tzu (Burton Watson, tr.)

In response to an invitation from the American Philosophical Association to present a paper on the general topic of interpretation at its annual meeting of the Eastern Division in 1981, I took the opportunity to extend and clarify the remarks on interpretation at the end of the preceding essay. I was unable to find a final argument against the respectability of deep interpretations, but it occurred to me that it was deep interpretations that those who argue against interpretation in art must have in mind: for deep interpreters always look past the work of art to something else. Of the many references in the piece, the Chiesa of Santo Leone Pietromontana may puzzle students of ecclesiastical architecture in Italy. There is of course no such church: the name is a rowdy translation into Italian of that of my friend, the art historian Leo Steinberg, whose neglected theory about moral diagonals in Michelangelo's Last Judgement *I wanted to celebrate. It was a present for him, and the essays are full of hidden presents—little examples calling in their own right for deep interpretation but needing none so far as just reading the text is concerned. But some readers will recognize something as put there just for her or him.*

THERE IS A concept of interpretation abroad these days which, though it arises in particular connection with texts, has little to do with matters that call for interpretation in the rather more routine acceptance of the term: with whether or not a certain ambiguity or inconsistency is intended and, if inadvertent, with how such flaws are to be resolved—with how the text is to be *read*. Thus the chronology appended by Faulkner to the text of *Abasalom, Absalom* happens to be inconsistent with the chronicle one may recover from the notoriously tortured narrative of the novel, and there is an initial question of whether Faulkner got it wrong or whether the text of the novel is to be amended, or if it was deliberately planted to excite an even deeper reflection on time, voice, and narration than the already complex narrative structure alone would arouse in the literary consciousness of the reader. More important, the chronology must on this latter interpretation be construed as part of a work which happens also to contain a narrative now perceived as a fragment: it belongs to a more complex literary object, like the arch index of *Pale Fire*, which recapitulates a mystery rather than helps the reader find his way about; and the identity of the work becomes indeterminate until a decision is made. Routine intrepretation is a matter of determining textual identity, then, and although any number of factors must be appealed to in support of a theory, the central and controlling hypothesis is to the likely representations of the author himself as to how the text is to be read. These representations, of course, would themselves have been subject to change, and we can imagine the inconsistency between chronicle and chronology brought to Faulkner's surprised attention, and that he decided to allow it to stand. A textual problem has then been resolved by incorporation, but the work has been altered from a somewhat conventional story in art deco prose to a modernist exercise in cross-generic self-consciousness, with a corresponding gain or loss in critical standing. The history of art and literature is filled with lost confrontational opportunities, so we shall never know for certain whether, for example,

Watteau's masterpiece *L'Embarquement à Cythère* displays its *triste* and ephemeral eroticists leaving, or leaving *for,* the Isle of Love—either reading being consistent with the language of the title but each requiring a different reading of the work, which in view of its ambiguity occupies a limbo in indeterminacy of the sort epitomized by the duck-rabbit of Vienna. As there is no end to critical speculation, there is no terminus to interpretation. But the concept of interpretation I am seeking to identify has little to do with this, though confusion between it and the textual labors of humanistic scholarship has tended to obscure the differences. *This* concept of interpretation belongs less to humane studies than to the *Geisteswissenschaften,* or to the *humansciences,* as I shall term them in an effort to preserve the German agglutinative. And these scorn reference to authorial representation altogether.

Neither, therefore, has it much to do with meaningful actions construed on the model of texts, at least when ambiguities and inconsistencies of a sort made inevitable by the open textures of speech and gesture demand an interpretation or make one possible. An action is meaningful when its description makes reference to a social institution or practice; so moving a stone for the mere sake of its spatial translation would not—whereas anything a king did as a king or because he is a king would—be a meaningful act. Charles VII made an exceedingly generous gesture to the Anglo-Burgundian garrison of Troyes when Joan of Arc took that city for him in the course of their triumphant coronation ride to Reims: he permitted them to leave, together with their arms and baggage. The Anglo-Burgundians cleverly if gracelessly interpreted "baggage" to include prisoners they had taken in hostage. Joan resisted this dilation of the term's extension, though a case would be made that prisoners held for ransom would be valuable property, that they owed their lives to their exchange value, that they literally had, like tents and *chaudières,* to be transported and, like horses, to be fed. Though this construction could scarcely have been intended by Charles, he in fact accepted the interpretation and ordered the ransoms paid. Whether he would have been that forthcoming had the Anglo-Burgundians proceeded to dilapidate Troyes, arguing that stones can be classed as arms if arrows are, since they are ammunition for catapults, is impossible now to determine. Yet, like Faulkner with *Absalom, Absalom* Charles stood in a position of authority over which interpretation(s) would be allowed, whatever may have been his precise intentions, and authority of this sort is always required when there is a system of distinctions—a language, a code, a teaching, a writ—which must be accommodated to circumstances for which it could not have been expressly designed.

Interpretation cannot be avoided if the system is to be flexible enough to work, and authority is demanded if it is not to go to such extremes of elasticity as no longer to *be* a system. So it is a matter of interpretation whether abortion is murder, whether it is rape when a man forces sex upon his reluctant wife, whether the theory of evolution is really a scientific theory, whether a revolutionary when captured is a criminal or to be treaded as a political prisoner, or whether a meaningful action is to be construed as a kind of text—and in each instance someone or something is an authority. The limits of interpretation would have been interpreted as the business, if not the essence, of philosophy not long ago, when what we say when, what we would say if, what we must say whether, were preemptively disputed in the analytical chambers of Oxford. And though neither here nor in the tribunal of social life is intention as such always invoked, what speakers or rulers might or must have meant, or would allow upon reflection were they consulted, is consistently appealed to as casuistry proceeds, and constitutes what most closely approaches experimental confirmation in such interpretational practice. So understanding what an author as agent and authority at once could have meant is central to this order of interpretation that *for just this reason*, must be distinguished from the sort of interpretation, hermeneutic or what I shall designate *deep* interpretation, which I want to examine here. It is deep precisely because there is not that reference to authority which is a conceptual feature of what we may as well term *surface* interpretation. There is not because the level of explanation referred to in deep interpretation is not a level on which a participant in a form of action can as such occupy a position of authority. Or the only authority that counts is that of the scientist, in this instance the humanscientist. The distinction would have been more intuitive at a time when science was not yet construed as merely another from of action, in which paradigms are contested in a manner not to be greatly differentiated from that in which missionaries and Melanesians contest over sexual moralities. The scientist does not make the realities he is authorative over and derive his authority from that, as an author or a ruler does—but this too can be a matter of philosophical litigation.

Perhaps a differentiation may be eked out as follows. The distinction between depth and surface cuts at right angles across the philosophically more commonplace distinction between inner and outer. It is difficult to draw the inner-outer distinction without begging every question in the philosophies of mind and knowledge, but surface interpretation undertakes to characterize the external behavior of an agent with reference to the internal representation of it presumed to be the agent's, and the agent is in some privileged position with regard to what his representations are. Or at least what his surface representations are. With regard to his deep representations, he has no privilege, hence no authority, for he must come to know them in ways no different from those imposed upon others: they are at least cognitively external to him, even if part of his character and personality, and with regard to them he is, as it were, an Other Mind to himself.

The operation know as *Verstehen*, in which we seek to interpret through vicarious occupation of the agent's own point of view, though certainly a flawed conception, is at least a possible theory of how the Outer traverses the dark boundaries that separate him from Inner, if we grant that Inner has no need or use for *Verstehen* as applied to himself, the point of view being his. But it is not a possible theory of how we arrive at a deep interpretation, if only because Inner is cut off from his own depths for reasons different from those that cut Outer off from Inner. It has been said that part of what makes a reason an unconscious one is that it would not be a reason for him whose action it explains if it were conscious. It would not in part because the beliefs that would justify it if conscious are alien to the system of beliefs which the agent would invoke. So it is part of something being deep that it is hidden, as much from him whose depth is in question as from anyone else. We may never—and bats may always—know what it is like to be a bat; but bats, if they have depths, are no better situated than we for knowing what it deeply is to be a bat. And perhaps the very notion of what it is to be something implies just that sort of consciousness which has no more application than the concept of authority to the depths. In the depths there is nothing that counts as being there.

Deep interpretation, all this having been said, cannot altogether dispense with those representations with reference to the accessibilty of which we mark the difference between Inner and Outer. It cannot because, in pretending to give a deep interpretation of what persons do, it takes it for granted that it is known what in fact persons do, and this may require reference precisely to those representations. Indeed, what deep interpretation undertakes is a kind of understanding of the complex consisting of representations together with the conduct they, at the surface level, enable us to understand; so surface interpretation, when successfully achieved, gives us the interpretanda for deep interpretation, the interpretantia for which are to be sought in the depths. So a deep reading of *Absalom, Absalom* seeks to interpret text and authorial representation together with reference to factors with regard to which it may be justifiably said that the interpreter knows things the author does not. Though an author, to the degree that he masters the technologies of deep interpretation, may come to be able to give deep interpretations of his own writings, he is in no better position to discern in these matters than anyone else, and questions of interpretation, in contrast with surface readings of the text, have nothing to do with questions on which he may be said to have some authority.

Surface interpretation, which we are all obliged in the course of socialization to become masters of, has been extensively discussed by philosophers in the theory of action and in the analysis of other languages and other minds. But deep interpretation has been scarcely discussed at all. Yet because it is practiced by the humansciences, the theories it presupposes are presupposed by them, and their viability depends upon its viabilty. I should like therefore to give some examples of deep interpretation and to sketch some problems it gives rise to in at least some of those examples. And I should like to dissipate certain confusions which come about, especially in the philosophy of art, when the claims of deep and surface interpretation are not kept isolated. Depth, needless to say, has little to do with profundity. But I have no analysis of "deep" in the sense of profound readings of texts to offer.

Of the forms of divination anciently practiced by the Greeks, one in particular has a curious pertinence to our topic. This was divination *dia kleodon,* exercised upon the casual utterances of men. The message-seeker pressed a coin into the hand of a certain statue of Hermes, whispered his query in the idol's ear, blocked his own ears—and the answer would be contained in the first human words he heard upon unblocking them. Needless to say, interpretation of these would be required, supposing, as altogether likely, the words did not transparently reveal the message. It would rarely have been as pointed as the text, randomly encountered on the surface but viewed as set there by Providence, that nudged Augustine onto the path of sainthood ("Not in rioting and drunkeness . . . "), nor as apt as the equally famous text from the *Confessions* ("And men go about to wonder at the heights of mountains . . . ") that Petrarch pretended to have come upon by accident while pondering his relationship to himself and history atop Mt. Ventoux. More likely a passerby mumbled something about the price of olive oil while the message-seeker wished to know whether Daphne (or was it Ion?) really cared. And an interpreter as middleman would be called upon to map interpretandum onto interpretans. The automatic writing from which the Surrealists sought to elicit astounding insights belongs to the same general sort of undertaking.

In view of the god's identity, we have an archeo-hermeneutical practice here, which pivots upon interpreting utterances "that mean more than the speaker realizes," which is the English definition of the Greek work *kledon*, herewith introduced as an English word in its own right. Divination, like oracles and auguries generally, has fallen into disuse, but kledons and the form of interpretation they exemplify play a considerable role in modern hermeneutic theory, where we deal with symbols that Ricoeur, somewhat gnomically, tells us "say more than they say." It is a kledon, then, when in saying a a speaker says b (or when, in performing a meaningful action c an agent does d), but where the ordinary structures for understanding a would not disclose to a hearer that b is also being said: nor is the speaker at all aware that he is saying b, meaning as he does only to be saying a (speakers have no authority over what they are saying when they voice kledons). In one of his novels, Vonnegut portrays a radio announcer in Nazi Germany who manages to alert the Allies to important military movements in Germany through messages coded into the anti-Semitic utterances his audience believes it is listening to. He happens to know he is doing this, which puts him in a difficult moral posture that would not be altered were he merely the writer of military intelligence embedded invisibly in bigoted discourse, delivered by a staff announcer who, unaware of hid-

den messages, would only be doing his job of filling the air
with banal evil. Like his ancient counterpart who was an
unwitting *porte-parole* of hermetic communication, this announcer would be kledonizing and, given his presumed values, would not transmit the concealed message if he knew he
was doing it; so what he is *deeply* doing is not only uninten-
tional, it is (almost dialectically) counterintentional. From
the perspective of the surface of discourse, the status as
kledon of what he says is inscrutable, and the meaning of
what he says in saying what he would suppose himself
(only) to be saying is not really his. Much as in one sense the
child born to the Virgin is not really *hers.* Had the identity
of the child not been somehow *revealed,* there would be no
way of knowing that a god had been born into history. It
takes a prophet to reveal the divine overcharge on ordinary
communication. Without these revelations, life would have
gone on in both instances with no way of knowing that
kledons were being transmitted into the unheeding air. What
makes kledons so interesting is that they supervene upon
forms of life and discourse that are already, as it were, under
surface interpretation complete as they are. It is like the
world being hidden in the world.

Now the interesting question is why the meanings are
hidden. We can of course understand it when the secret
agent uses the airwaves to disguise subversive intelligence,
but why must Hermes graft his tidings onto inadvertent hosts
instead of speaking directly? Well, why must Jupiter have
recourse to bolts of lightning and flights of birds to communicate matters it would not have been thought beyond divine
power to lay upon us directly, without the mediation of interpreters? There is a cynical answer. If there were direct communication, the interpreters would suffer technological un-
employment. So in order to secure their economic position,
they claim semantical monopoly over crucial urgent messages that only they can make out. I have no idea whether
this cynical answer is true, but it illustrates a kind of low-
level deep interpretation in its own right, in that the di-

vinators are in fact maintaining their own position in the world through the fact that their clients believe them to be discharging an important, though in truth it is an epiphenomenal, function. The deep reasons governing these transactions, and in the light of which we are enabled to say what really is happening, are hidden from interpreter and consumer alike, and the surface practice would not survive if the deep reasons for it were known: it would not exist if it were *not* hidden. Its being hidden from the client could be put down as priestly fourberie but for the fact that it is hidden from the priests themselves: which is what makes the mechanisms of concealment philosophically interesting.

I have archeologized this long-abandoned practice to bring to prominence a structure of action in which, when *a* is done, there is a description of *a*, call it *b*, such that in doing *a*, one is really doing *b* in the sense that *a* is done in order that *b* be done—which distinguishes *b* from the countless many other descriptions of *a* recognized in the theory of action—and where it is hidden from the *a*-doer that he is a *b*-doer. A deep interpretation of *a* identifies it as *b*. Surface interpretation, as we saw, is with reference to the agent's reasons, though not his deep reasons, and though he may have difficulty in saying what his reasons are, this will not be because they are hidden. Its being hidden is a special kind of reason for not being able to make something out. But let me now give some examples, most of them familiar, where it seems to me this structure occurs.

Marxist Theories

Marx and Engels do not accept at face value the descriptions and explanations men spontaneously give of their own actions. In every instance this side of the classless society, in doing *a*, whatever it may be, they are doing something else, call it *b*, which must be understood in terms of their class location. Marx explained the repeal of the Corn Laws, under

the ideological leadership of Cobden and the political leadership of Peel, which *they* explained as done in order that the
working man should pay less for bread, as *really* to be explained as done so that the industrialist should pay less for
the working man. Peel and Cobden, both Free Traders, vested
their actions (sincerely) in humanitarian terms, but really
were advancing the interests of their class, just as their oppo-
nents were expressing the interests of theirs. Peel was politically and Cobden economically ruined, but they were but
the kledons of their class, instruments of the forces of history
in the dramatical interplay of which classes are the true
agents. A parallel sort of theory explains the sacrifice of the
male insect in the rage of reproduction in terms of the interests of the species.

Nonlogical Behavior

The economic principles of the Liberal reformers of
1846 define one of the few examples Pareto is disposed to
regard as *logical,* namely pursuing one's own interests. But
much of what men do is nonlogical, in the repect that the
explanations men give of what they do is in reality no explanation at all, and underlying a whole class of actions is what
Pareto terms a *residue,* which really explains what the *de facto*
explanations men give only rationalize. Pareto-interpretation
seeks the residue underlying conduct and rationalization together. A man forbears from murder because he has a deep
horror of murder, but he explains forbearance with reference
to his fears that the gods will punish him. Etc., etc., etc.

Psychoanalytical Theories

Pareto says rather little about what residues are or how
they are to be explained, being content to identify with the
zeal of the village atheist the countless pieces of nonlogical

conduct that "originate chiefly in psychic states, sentiments, subconscious feelings, and the like." A better theory comes from Freud. The distance between a commonplace and a kledonic reading of an action or an utterance could scarcely have been more surprising under divination *dia kleodon* than the distance between the manifest thought or conduct of a person and its redescription with reference to its latent form as revealed by psychoanalytical interpretation. The Ratman jogs furiously after meals, "in order," he would rationalize, patting a surprisingly flat stomach, "to eliminate *Dick*." *Dick*, which is thickness in the Ratman's native language, German, happens also to be the name of his lady-love's American suitor, whose elimination the Ratman deeply intends. Obviously, jogging cannot remotely be a means for eliminating rivals, and "eliminating Dick" would not be a reason for running were it conscious. So the acceptable reason, "in order to eliminate *Dick*," only rationalizes a reason the Ratman cannot acceptably act on and connects with this deep reason via a punning transformation; and the deep reason is hidden from him, though not from his interpreter (Freud), for whatever reason the unconscious itself is hidden. The example is far from atypical, and the type is found broadcast through Freud's collected works.

Structuralisms

Puns plan transformative roles in Freud's great hermeneutical works, which may explain, if those works are sound, why puns are socially so offensive (why do they meet with groans, why are they classed the "lowest form of humor," why does the leading French philosogist, who has made punning the principal feature of his mythod, get rejected for positions in his ungrateful land?), and certainly explains, since puns are native to the language they occur in, why they cannot be translated. So interpretation, rather than translation or even paraphrase, connects the speech and actions of the neuropath to the Language of his Unconscious. Indeed it is just because the symptom is a pun on the psychic pathogen that Lacan postulates his hasty theory that the structure of the unconscious must be the structure of a language. Psychoanalysis as practiced by Lacan consists precisely in identifying what the symptom says—or better, what a piece of behavior says when treated as a symptom, where symptoms are treated as a discourse hidden, as it were, on the surface of conduct, as the purloined letter is hidden in full sight of those who seek it. But the theory of the linguistic unconscious generates a wide class of theories—e.g., Lévi-Strauss' witty thought that marriage is a kind of language, or at least a form of communication, if we can construe, as he sees no obstacle to doing, the exchange of women as a kind of exchange of words. Now the reasons Elizabeth may give for marrying Paul are rationalizations of the interests of clans she is *really* advancing, whatever *she* may think. Dinners at the Douglases', cockfights at the Geertzes', are other examples of conduct in which whatever we think we are doing, we are doing something else, deep interpretation telling us what.

Philosophies of History

It is Hegel who lays upon us the alarming thought that "Reason is the sovereign of the world," and that "the history of the world, therefore [*sic*], presents us with a rational process." So, however chaotic it may appear, Reason is in some way to be interpreted as acting through the actions of men to achieve ends, or an end, which can come about in no other way, even though the secondary agents of historical realization are totally unaware of the grand scheme in which they figure. What Hegel speaks of as Reason is close to what Vico speaks of as Providence, which exploits human intentions in order to subvert them and bring about states of affairs ironically opposite to what those who act on those intentions

envision. Through "ferocity, arrogance, and ambition . . . the three great vices that could detroy mankind on
the face of the earth" are generated "soldiers, merchants,
and rulers," through the civilizing conduct of whom social
happiness prevails. The kledonic meaning of actions under
the interpretational schemes of philosophical history are hidden from agents for whatever reason the future is hidden.

These are perhaps examples enough. I want now briefly
to comment on some structural features they share.

It is difficult to know whether more to admire the an-
tique divinators for having grasped a structure repeatedly
exhibited in some of the most influential humansciences of
modernist times, or to suspect these latter hermeneutical enterprises for finding cognitive satisfaction in structures from
a more ignorant and credulous age. Or to draw some inferences from the fact that we may have turned up a residue,
in Pareto's sense, and that each of these humansciences owes
its existence to an impulse, also realized in biblical interpretation, to get answers of a certain kind to questions that
ought not to be put. But I hesitate to offer a deep interpretation of deep interpretation, not merely because I have some
serious reservations about an enterprise no less suspicious
when exercised upon itself in self-deconstruction, but because I wish to show how easy it is to avoid the dread Hermeneutical Circle, namely by refusing to step into it, avoid-
ing hermeneutics altogether.

Instead I should like to bring out some conceptual features of the humansciences by drawing a contrast with a
quite different account altogether of human conduct, namely
that kind of token materialism which holds that mental states
are really states of our neural system—a theory I mention
rather than describe because of the general familiarity of that
sort of theory to philosophers. There is, I think, no temptation to say that this is an interpretive theory (though of
course there is a sense of interpretation which is virtually

synonymous with theory), nor that we *interpret* mental states in terms of neural states. In part this is because we know very little about neural states, let along enough to say with which neural states this or that mental state is to be identified, whereas the terms used to describe interpretantia in the deep humansciences are mainly very familiar to us, with definite analogies to distinctions on the surface—e.g., we refer to deep interests, desires, feelings, beliefs, strategies, and the like. But the contrast is sharper than this, I think, and I would like to make a few observations to the end of revealing the differences between a natural science, as it were, of human conduct and humanscience.

First, materialist theories, if redeemed by scientific ones, would be universal in the sense of allowing no exceptions, a claim which must immediately be qualified to accommodate functionalistic possibilities that mental states which in human are identified with neural states should in other orders of creatures be differently embodied. But at least no unembodied mental state is allowed. Deep theories in the humansciences allow, on the other hand, a great many exceptions, so it is not true that every surface phenomenon really has a deep interpretation. The deep structures of class membership and class conflict evaporate in the classless society in which men become coincident with what for lack of a contrast can no longer be termed their surface selves. Pareto allows that not all conduct is nonlogical and traceable to residues, and conceivably he drew attention to residues to liberate us from their distorting energies. Freud surely did not believe that all behavior was neurotic, to be referred via interpretation to unresolved conflicts in the unconscious, and in any case the possibility of a cure promised a form of integrated being suspiciously similar to that promised when class conflicts are resolved (though Freud was pessimistic about cures and it is in fact exceedingly difficult to find out whether he really cured anyone). Hegel excluded certain events from what we may as well call deep history—e.g., what happens in Siberia has no historical meaning whatever. And, lest we forget, only the first utterance heard by the message-seeker is a kledon. I am less certain whether structuralisms allow exceptions, though to the degree that it is possible that there should be actions that are not meaningful actions, it is possible that there are actions for which no deep interpretation is in order. The repertoire of actions somewhat narrowly addressed by recent action theorists—raising an arm, moving a stone— could be nonmeaningful in principle when nothing ulterior is done by doing these beyond what simply here is said to be done—raising an arm, moving a stone. So these may occur outside any structures at all. By similar reckoning, not every even meaningful utterance is a speech-act—viz., covered by rules of a certain sort such that, in saying *s*, one may be interpreted as doing *d*. Thus meaningful utterance need not have the kind of meaning described by structuralist theories.

Secondly, there is no inclination to say that a given mental state *means*, or refers to, the neural state it is identical with if the theory is true, but the very use of the expression "interpretation" implies just that in connecting surface with depth. The interpreter tells us what deep thing a surface thing means. It is this semantical component in the theories of the humansciences which distinguishes them in part from those of the natural sciences and which licenses the characterization of surface phenomena as in some sense like language. Contemporary anthropology has enabled us to see the most banal or at least commonplace actions as part of a communication system, so no one can any longer flatly describe ordering a meal, building a house, shopping for clothes, or launching a seduction in the flat terms of food, shelter, warmth, and sex. And it is with reference to a system of meanings which penetrates existence very deeply indeed that we interpret phenomena whose surface interpretations may be quite different.

Finally, it seems to me that deep interpretantia are intensional for just the reason that makes them deep, namely that they can afford descriptions of the same phenomena covered by surface interpretation, and that it is false that the descriptions are deep in the terms used by surface interpretation.

This would make sense if in fact the deep interpretantia were representations, for intensionality has to do precisely with representing representations. So the humansciences refer us to various representational systems with reference to which what humans do is to be understood, though those whose representations these are will naturally not be conscious of them as *their* representations. And in some cases they could not rationally allow them. Dotty as he was, the Ratman could hardly consciously suppose himself to be representing himelf as eliminating a rival by running after meals. But in any case it is far from plain that neural states have representational properites or that neural sciences are intensionalistic at all. But these are matters better discussed elsewhere.

Whatever the case, it should be clear what deep interpretation consists in, at least in part. Surface occurrences stand in two distinct relationships to depth occurrences. We interpret s in terms of d when s means d and when d explains s. Moreover, d is a representation on the part of him whose surface behavior is being interpreted; but, typically, that he represents the world under d is hidden from him. The comparison with materialism has allowed these features to emerge, and at this point I drop the comparison. Needless to say, it was not drawn with invidious intent, nor meant as indicating failings in the humansciences. What have in fact been regarded as failings may have arisen only because an inappropriate model of a quite different sort of science has been applied to them, and the differences noted may serve to help draw that boundary between the humansciences and the nature-sciences dimly discriminated by theorists in the early twentieth century. That will be a task for another time. I would now like to dispel a confusion I am far better equipped to deal with, namely one which has clouded the philosophy of art when features of deep interpretation have been the basis for drawing inappropriate inferences about the interpretation of works of art.

In view of the fact that any work of art you choose can

be imagined matched by a perceptually congruent counterpart which, though not a work of art, cannot be told apart
from the artwork by perceptual differentia, the major problem in the philosophy of art consists in identifying what the
difference then consists in between works of art and mere
things. Consider thus the corpus of Leonardo's frescoes
viewed in the light of a curious bit of advice he offered fellow
painters as a stimulant to invention. He urges them to equip
themselves with a wall spotted with stains. Then, whatever
they intend to paint, they will find pictorial adumbrations of
it on the smudged wall. "You will see in it a resemblance to
various landscapes, adorned with mountains, rivers, rocks,
trees, plains, wide valleys, and various groups of hills. You
will also be able to see divers combats and figures in quick
movement and strange expressions of faces and outlandish
costumes, and an infinite number of things you can reduce
into separate and well-conceived forms." (Leonardo observes that similarly every tune can be heard in pealing bells,
and I am certain that there is a literary equivalent where
every story can be read from a patch of spotted prose.) There
are sheets of Leonardo's sketches that may have been generated by just such transfigurative vision, and it is always fascinating to speculate over which of his great works may have
been provoked into artistic existence by this prosthetic of
painterly vision. But this suggests an obverse exercise—to try
to see, through an act of deliberate *disinvention*, a divine
landscape, such as the one against which la Gioconda is set,
or for that matter La Gioconda herself, as so much stain-
splotched expanse. Nature and a certain surprising casual-
ness regarding the material bases of his craft have helped
turn certain of Leonardo's works into what looks like stains
to the casual eye. His *intonacco* for the *Battle of Anghiari* was,
Vasari tells us, so coarse that the legendary composition sank
into the wall; and though recent projects have thought of
locating it by means of sonar and thus bringing a lost masterpiece to light, it is conceivable that the wall was stuccoed
over in the first place because it looked more and more as

though it were attacked by mildew. The rough napoleonic troops who occupied the refectory in Milan where the *Last Supper* is painted are often impugned as barbarians for the brutal way they treated that priceless wall, but since it takes strenuous curatorial intervention even today to prevent the painting from subsiding into stains, it is feasible that the soldiers only saw it as so much fungus and damp. To be sure, there may here to there have been seen a surprising form— an eye, a finger—but that might itself be of the same playful order as seeing the profile of Talleyrand in a lombardian cloud or, more likely in terms of soldierly fantasy, two hills as *des tetons*.

So imagine that on a forgotten wall in the sacristy of the Chiesa of Santo Leone Pietromontana, Leonardo depicted a Last Judgement that has, alas, reverted to a set of stains so as to be indiscernible from the very wall in Leonardo's studio from which his fancy projected and realized those great works, including, of course, the Last Judgement itself. Both have a certain art-historical interest. Owning the wall in the studio would be like owning Leonardo's palette, or better, his *camera obscura*. It would be owning a bit of remarkable gear. Owning the other wall, by contrast, would be owning a work of art in a sad state of degradation, worth, even so, plenty of millions if only the *Patrimonio Nazionale* would permit it to be moved to Düsseldorf or Houston. Knowing it to be a work of art, we must interpret those stains and mottles, an operation having no application to the counterpart, though we may use the latter just as Leonardo did, to excite the visual imagination. To interpret means in effect an imaginative restoration, to try to find the identity of areas gone amorphous through chemistry and time. It would be helpful to have a sketch, a contemporary copy, a description—anything to help with recovering Leonardo's intentions. There are many Last Judgements, but how much really will they help us? Will this one possess the celebrated moral diagonal the Vatican guides never tire of tracing for the edification of tourists who learned about it through popular lectures on Michelangelo? Will there even be a Christ figure? Perhaps Leonardo absented Him from a scene defined by His traditionally heavy presence. Or perhaps a certain blob is all that remains of a remarkable Christ, originally tiny in proportion to the dimension of the tableau, one more anticipation to Leonardo's credit, this time to manneristic optics. Interpretations are endless, but only because knowledge is unattainable. The right sort of knowledge gives the work its identity, and *surface* interpretation has done its work. What remains is responding to the work, so far as this is possible in its sad state. We have an aesthetic for ruins, even for faded photographs, but not quite for ruined paintings. But such matters must be mooted elsewhere.

Deep interpretation supposes surface interpretation to have done its work, so that we know what has been done and why. Now we look for the deep determinates of da vincian action. Appeal to his intentions only individuates the interpretandum for a deep interpretation, but the interpretantia refer us to Leonardo's kinky unconscious, his economic locus, and to the semiotics of embellishment in Florentine culture—what the Medici went in for instead of cockfights—and on and on and on. There is no end to deep interpretation, perhaps because there is no end to science, not even humanscience, and who knows what deep structures the future will reveal? The artist's intentions have nothing to do with these. Surface interpretation must be scrupulously historical, and refer only to possibilities Leonardo could have acknowledged without attributing to him knowledge of the humansciences of the future. He could not have known of Eisler's book, nor the theory Eisler used. But that requires no references to the artist's authority. Deep interpretation, finally, admits a certain overdetermination—the work can mean many different things under deep interpretation without being rendered the least indeterminate under surface interpretation. Like philosophy, in a way, deep interpretation leaves the world as it finds it. Nor does knowledge of it enter into response, except to the degree that response itself is given deep interpretation.

It is deep interpretation which those who speak out against interpretation speak out against, in urging that we allow the works to speak for themselves. They hardly can be speaking out against surface interpretation, inasmuch as we cannot so much as identify the work, let alone allow it to speak, save against an assumption of achieved interpretation. Without surface interpretation, the artworld lapses into so much ruined canvas, and so many stained walls.

Of course it is irresistable to ponder what need for ritual purification it must have been that drove Leonardo to transcend stains and transfigure them into works of art—to ask what the stains *meant*—and to contrast his achievement with that of the American painter Morris Louis, in whose works stains remain stains, resist transfiguration even into veils, showing, perhaps, a hatred for fat? a need to soil? a wish for pushing off the white radiance of eternity? . . . This is to treat works of art as Leonardo treated his spotted wall, as an occasion for critical invention which knows no limit, the deep play of departments of literature and hermeneutics.

IV.

Language, Art, Culture, Text

For a work of art to be a work
of art, it must rise above
grammer and syntax.
> —Barnett Newman

This piece was in response to an invitation to participate in a plenary session of the World Congress of Philosophy, held August 1983 in Montreal. My task was to speak on art, language, and culture, in twenty minutes. In truth it is easier to speak on all three than on any one of them alone, and I facilitated my task even further by adding a fourth item, that of the text. The latter is taken up again in Essay VII and has, I believe, deep implication for the philosophy of mental representations I have been elaborating elsewhere. In any case, this essay enabled me to clarify the sense in which interpretation must be relativized to a culture, without this entailing any damaging relativistic thesis about art: its cultural locus is among the factors that enter into a work's identity. That the concept of a text should cut across the distinction between pictorial depiction and verbal description may be kept in mind when I later engage the specific difficulties in distinguishing philosophical from non-philosophical texts, in order to resist the assimilation of philosophy to art. The essay appeared under the title "Art and Text" in Res, *thanks to Francesco Pellizzi.*

STUDENTS OF ZEN are bound to be familiar with the ten Ox-herding pictures, with their sequential representation of a certain spiritual itinerary, and hence with the eighth picture (figure 1), which is simply an empty circle, located just after a picture of the Ox-herd in a posture of contemplation (figure 2) and just before an affecting landscape (figure 3) dense with the absence of any human form. The empty circle makes the seventh picture (figure 2) ambiguous, at least initially, since there is in it a circle in the sky, which could of course be the moon and read as such were one to see the picture in isolation, but could also represent the impending enlightenment, or *satori*, which is actualized in print Eight: so one has to determine whether Eight, in addition to its obvious reference, refers, intratextually, as it were, to this part of Seven, if one is to get a clear interpretation. Eight, in any case, is a picture of Enlightenment, of a certain blankness—and one must, as my late friend Shiko Munakata would have said, distinguish the blankness of the paper from the blankness of the picture—but its being a *circle* appears to play no cognitive role, not being part of what is meant. We are not dealing here with a kind of geometrical mysticism of

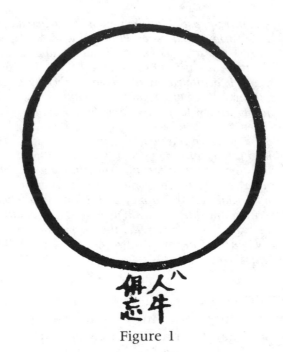

Figure 1

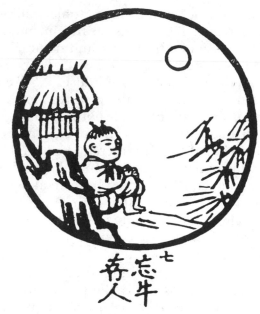

忘牛七
齐人

Figure 2

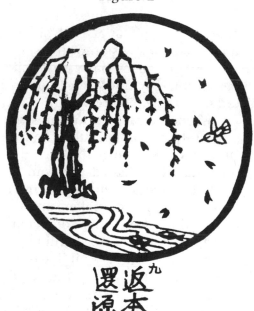

返本九
還源

Figure 3

the sort characteristic in the neoplatonic tradition in the
West, the sort which Ficino has clearly in mind when he
claims that "because of a necessary and natural instinct . . .
every mind praises the round figure when it first encounters
it in things, and knows not why it praises it." We know this
because all ten of the Ox-herding pictures are composed in
circular frames, so circularity adds nothing to number Eight,
when, though an empty circle, is not of a circular emptiness.
It is rather that kind of total undifferentiated blank we associate with Buddhist imagery, and so an indiscernible figure in
some neoplatonic sequence would have an altogether different meaning, which would differ again from a vastly more
ambiguous circle, whether empty or not we cannot say, since
it might be a disk, and whether a work or not we cannot say,
since it might be only a diagram.

We could only say these things on the basis of informa-
tion that nothing compassed by the psychology of pictorial
perception can disclose. Pictorial psychology, for example,
cannot instruct us as to whether the circle in the seventh Ox-
herding picture is the moon, in which case its edges are the
moon's edges and it is a pictorial part of the picture; or
whether it is an anticipatory vision of the state depicted in
Eight, in which case its edges have no relationship with
those of its subject, which in any case has none, and it is not
so much a pictorial part as a picture-within-a-picture, standing in complex psychological relationships with the rapt
Ox-herd himself. Only an independent knowledge of the
concept of *satori* makes this particular pictorial knowledge
possible, and this must be squared with our knowledge of
the pictorial possibilities of the culture the work belongs to—
whether, for example, its picture-makers and their audience
had attained to the kind of pictorial competence shown in
our own comic strips, which the Ox-herding pictures so interestingly resemble. Print Eight is a bit like the familiar *Pow!*
that occurs in a balloon above the overpowered one's head,
or in a frame of its own.

Blank and *of* blank as the eighth Ox-herding picture is,

its powerful impact on the viewer—or reader—is connected
with the fact that it represents a change into a spiritual state
of the highest importance, and it seems plain to me that
without some understanding of the theory of enlightenment,
of the urgency attached to its attainment, and of the fact that
it is an episode in a life—as print Nine makes explicit—rather
than a terminal culmination, one cannot feel the power of
print Eight, or even respond to it as powerful. One might
compare it with the nearest counterpart I can think of in
our own tradition, the twelfth panel in Barnett Newman's
fourteen-panel *The Stations of the Cross*. In it there is a sudden
reversal of color, as though whatever itinerary the series represents had reached some critical and especially somber
point, since panel Twelve is dominantly black, whereas the
preceding panels are white, indeed blank canvas, with black
stripes or, as Newman called them, "zips." The black in panel
Twelve is too dominating and wide for the area it fills to be
thought of as a stripe—and it seems iconographically wrong
to think of it as a zip. It is difficult to imagine an exact
correspondence between the fourteen panels and the traditional stations of the cross: we are not looking at
Domenichino, after all, and Newman himself says that "it is
not the terrible walk up the Via Dolorosa" which he was
seeking to show. He nevertheless gave the panels sequential
identifications from the tradition, and it comes as no surprise
to learn that panel Twelve is *The Death of Christ*. It comes as
no surprise, that is, if one has been following the sequence
and then *comes* to Twelve: for it must represent the sort of
change of state the entire concept of the story of Christ promises as possible. This meaning quite evaporates, and along
with it the power of the work, if we bracket the panel by
imagining it separated from the others, or even imagine it
part of the entire series but experienced by someone who
does not know that these are stations of the cross, or does not
know what the stations of the cross are. And of course it
would be possible for someone to stigmatize panel Twelve as
empty, not in the spiritual sense of the eighth Ox-herding

print, with its allusions to the blank scriptures of Tripitika or
the equally blank wall before which the Boddidharma got
what he got, but in the routine aesthetic or critical sense of
the term which came so easily to those who first saw Newman's work, even in the New York artscene when it was
finally possible for it to exist. It would incidentally be *false* of
this particular work of Newman's, as it might be true of some
other panel exactly like it, by Newman or someone else,
Clyfford Still perhaps, which had a different meaning, or
which pretended, as a bare abstraction, to have none.

Charles Lamb, writing of the engravings of Hogarth,
says, "Other pictures we look at, his was read." And indeed
those deeply narrative, not to say moralistic, pictures have to
be worked out in a detail to match the detail of the individual
engravings, to a point where giving a reading of Hogarth
could become, as it did, a genre of interpretative literature. I
am certain that working through the prints is part of what
experiencing the prints consists in, that they are meant to
transform the reader through his identification of the sordid
stories they depict. The engravings make some narrative references back and forth in such a way that the order of the
prints in narrative time would control the interpretation, if
working through the prints means working through the
story. If the print showing the Harlot's death, for example, or
the Rake's death, came first in the actual order—numbered
"One" say—what came next would be a flashback, and one
would have to speculate why such a narrative strategy as that
which required the invention of narrative cinema should
have been precociously anticipated here. Why the time *in*
and the time *of* the narrative film need at times to work
against one another belongs to a different discussion, but my
immediate point is that there is an ideal order to Hogarth's
engravings, as there is to *The Stations of the Cross* or the Ox-
herding pictures. I have a set of the latter which goes in
actual fact from back to front, but this is not a factor to be
taken into interpretive account, not belonging to the work,
as it were, but to the book, since Japanese books, whether

the text is pictorial or not, are to be read back to front. In any case, part of the reason that Hogarth's engravings are to be read is that their natural context is narrative, and working through the narrative is presupposed if the response is to be as intended. Admittedly a single engraving would not be as radically diminished if isolated from context as the eighth Ox-herding picture would be; it would look narrative in a way that the twelfth station of the cross does not, but even so reference and structure are sufficiently interconnected in these highly representationalist works that even they would suffer truncation and distortion if on their own. They have, like their optically simpler counterparts, what meaning they do have only in the *Zusammenhang* of a larger statement.

"Have what meaning they do have only in the *Zusammenhang* of a larger statement" is a phrase, however vague, which has been chosen to sound an echo with a famous formulation in Frege, itself so much a part of philosophical culture that my implied audience may be as much counted on to hear it through my text as Newman's could be counted on to know roughly what the stations of the cross were and prepared to see black paint as a suitable metaphor for death, as *becoming* black was a suitable metaphor for dying, or as the intended readers of the Ox-herding pictures could appreciate a blank space as an appropriate image for enlightenment. I labor to make explicit what I am also supposing will be a spontaneous connection, in part because I want to illustrate the sort of connection I need, but in part to reject a closer analogy with the specific sort of meaning-conferring context Frege had in mind: the context of the sentence. For the structure of a work is not the structure of a sentence, and the understanding of a work is not even parallel to the grammatical competence engaged by the production and understanding of the sentences in one's language. Our theme is language, art, and culture, and my effort here is to draw philosophical attention to an order of context, of *Zusammenhang*, which is minimally required by the existence of art.

A great deal of energy today is carried by the concept of

the *text*, which transcends, in ways not yet made adequately clear, the basic unit of linguistic transmission, the least bearer of truth-values, the *sentence*, which Frege is deservedly given credit for having made primary. Now the primacy of the sentence (or the proposition, as in the present *Zusammenhang* it does not matter) has more or less defined analytical philosophy, with its strong emphasis upon the philosophies of language and of logic, and where the main recent division has been between those for whom a sentence is an instrument in the facilitation of a language game, or something to be understood through the conditions under which it is true, or some combination of these. This has made it virtually impossible for analysts to engage in discussion with philosophers, preeminently Continental, whose basic unit is the text. A text is a *Zusammenhang*, the principle of whose integrity goes beyond those features of syntax and grammar through which sentences are logically tractable, and through which sentences are held together in those larger architectures that have been the preeminent concerns of philosophical analysis—the argument and the logical calculus—whose function is the preservation and transmission of truth-values. A recent series of studies is entitled "The Arguments of the Philosophers," but one titled instead the *texts* of the philosophers would call for methods of an order we barely have glimpsed, these being the as yet unarticulated methods of interpretation. It was by dint of an implied interpretation, which it would be the task of a reader to recover, that the blank circle in the Ox-herding pictures is artistically identified as *satori* or as the Ox-herd having attained it: and its being in this sense *satori* is not (sounding another allusion) in the text in the way in which a word is in a sentence.

In saying that a text conforms to principles different from those which bind words into a sentence, I am allowing, of course, that a text could consist of a single sentence, or even a fragment of one, much in the same way in which a sentence could consist of a single word. The unit sentence consisting of the word *t* has meanings in excess of the meanings of *t* alone, as the text consisting of the unit sentence *s* will have. It is obvious that I cannot here do much to bring to explicitness what one might portentously call textual logic, but I would like to say that its principles cut across the differences between pictorial texts, of the sort I have been considering, and texts which happen in fact to be composed of sentences and ultimately of words. It is that the relationships between words and then between sentences in the *Zusammenhang* of a text go beyond grammar and syntax. There are differences between pictorial and linguistic representations which count heavily against the possibility of a purely pictorial language of the sort fantasized by Wittgenstein in the *Tractatus,* but at the level of text these differences disappear, which is why it is not even a stretched metaphor to say that Hogarth's engravings are to be *read.* A text, pictorial or verbal, begins to claim the status of art when certain questions arise in connection with it which cannot, on the one side, be answered through optics or pictorial psychology; or simply being able to read or just to be able to follow a text, say a narrative text, on the other.

Consider, for example, the last word in *Ulysses,* which is of course the word Yes, capitalized as in our notation only proper names or the beginnings of sentences are, but which is not itself a proper name and, having no period after it, is probably not a sentence either. Molly's soliloquy is filled with yeses, but none of them is marked in the way in which this terminal Yes is, and those who have to read this text aloud, like Siobhan McKenna, have to give some interpretation of this differentiated affirmative, the question being how it is to *sound,* granting that Molly is not speaking out loud— though if the Yes marked some kind of orgasm she *might* have voiced it as an ecstatic moan. Whatever the case, one cannot simply read *Ulysses* without countless questions of this sort arising: why is the Yes capitalized, the answer having also to explain why all the letters in it are not capitalized, and does it matter that this is Molly's final word in terms of her relationship to Bloom, to whom her *first* word in the novel was the uncommitting *Mn* in response to his question of whether she wanted something for breakfast: it leaves

Bloom with the question of interpretation amplified for us by the final ringing Yes. It is plain that we cannot really even say what happens in *Ulysses* without giving answers to questions of this order, so that a dense mediation of interpretation stands between the book and the work. It should not be difficult to show exactly the same sorts of considerations arising in connection with music, so that at the level of textual interpretation, differences between music, literature, and painting, which seem so frustrating at a lower level of analysis, give way to the possibility of a general method of interpretation. It in any case helps show how literature, though made of language, is defined by forces beyond the reach of grammatical and syntactical structure. It also shows why reading of the sort involving interpretation calls on skills of a sort different from those transmitted in teaching children to read, say, English.

Interpretation is the agency of what I have spoken of as transfiguration, that process whereby even quite commonplace objects are raised to the level of art. It remains such an agency when the objects to be transfigured already have the status of representational objects, such as pictures or pieces of descriptive writing, since not every picture is a work of art, nor every piece of prose. Indeed, not every piece of music is either, for only when questions parallel to those I have been raising arise for music are we at the level of art, for to treat something as a work of art is to suppose that it falls under the structure of interpretation. When the objects already are symbols of some order, then interpretation involves a very complex interplay between their use and their mention, so to speak, in that what a symbol means in the *Zusammenhang* of a text cannot be said until, in addition to its use, we answer such questions about its palpable features as those we asked in connection with the inscribed Yes in *Ulysses,* or the circular form of the eighth Ox-herding picture, which proved textually irrelevant though it might seem as though it should not be. Its irrelevancy has to be decided by appeal to other features of the text as well as of the culture from which the text comes and to which it primarily belongs.

It is because of these palpable features in excess of the features which make for semantical analysis that a work of art, even when straightforward narrative, cannot be collapsed onto its content: there is something in the telling of the story which is more than the story told. It is for these reasons that even when a work of art is, as critics and literary theorists loosely say, "referential," it is never merely referential. For these reasons I speak of works of art as semi-opaque objects.

By a semi-opaque object, I mean one which presents a content, but where the mode of presentation—once more a fregean notion—must be compounded with the content to determine the meaning of the object. There is a rhetorical dimension to any work of art in consequence of this interplay between content and mode of presentation, for the details of which I must refer the reader to *The Transfiguration of the Commonplace,* but it is internally connected with the psychology of artistic response, in which interpretation is coimplicated with appreciation. But it is equally connected with the concept of style, understood in terms of the interplay between content and mode. Here, for example, is Denis Donahue on Elizabeth Hardwick on Thomas Mann: "She writes that 'He combined the purest gifts with the earthbound consent, of a distinguished old dray horse, to pull heavy loads,' a sentence in which a heavy load is pulled mainly by the combined force of two commas." If a decision has to be made, at the level of punctuation, using two commas myself to refer to two commas in Miss Hardwick's sentence, then it is plain that interpretation must be a long and fastidious enterprise, and one which all by itself justifies the existence of critics such as Hardwick and Donahue. There is a lighthearted view abroad these days that a text is the infinite possibility of interpretation, that of any given text infinite interpretations can be given, none definitive. If two commas have to be decided, just giving *one* interpretation is enterprise enough.

There is a speculative question of the greatest urgency, as to whether the intricate constitution of a work of art gives us an analogy to the way in which students of a culture must constitute that culture anthropologically. This scarcely can be considered without pressing the question of inhowfar there is an analogy between cultures and works of art—a translation effected with the easy insouciance of genius by Burkhardt in treating the state "as a work of art" in his study of the Renaissance. To carry the analogy through, one would have to decide in the first place whether a culture might be regarded as a mode of presenting the world to its own members—a *Weltanschauung,* as we say—and hence already has a kind of representational content. One would then have to show the sort of interplay between that content and its mode of representation, which then constitutes, so to say, the style of the culture. This is to invert a celebrated saying of Wittgenstein, in this case to imagine a form of life being to imagine a language. By a language here, of course, I mean a system of representations rather than a system of uses, or it is to understand the system of uses as a set of symbols through which the members of a culture live their way of representing the world. It then would be the task of interpretation to decide which of the many day-to-day activities of the members of the culture carry this expressive overcharge. Even in works of art, as we saw, not everything belonging to the object belongs to the work. I do not know, for example, whether the alliteration "distinguished old dray horse" works together with the two commas, or not.

I scarcely could hope to carry the analogy further here, or perhaps anywhere, and not just for reasons of time. But if it has any chance at truth, artistic criticism becomes a paradigm of what we might now call cultural criticism, and the philosophical structure of the cultural sciences will then be so different from what those who framed the division between the *Natur-* and the *Geisteswissenschaften* had in mind by the latter that we hardly have any idea of what such sciences involve. We have no idea yet of what the humansciences are to be like, hence no idea of what it means finally to be human if participation in such forms is to be a condition of that—no idea, that is to say, save what guidance we may derive from the philosophy of art and the structures it has begun to bring to light.

V.

The End of Art

Art is dead.
Its present movements are not at all indications of vitality;
they are not even the convulsions of agony prior to death;
they are the mechanical reflex actions of a corpse submitted to galvanic force.
> —Marius de Zayas, "The Sun Has Set,"
> *Camera Work* (July 1912), 39:17.

This essay grew out of a brief contribution to a symposium on the state of the artworld and published, with comparable statements by John Berger, Clement Greenberg, and Rosalind Krauss, under the witty title "Art Attacks" in the lamented Soho News. *On the basis of that statement, I was invited to the Walker Institute for Contemporary Art in Minneapolis, to present one in a series of lectures on the future. That lecture was expanded considerably to form the target contribution to a volume, edited by Berel Lang and published by Haven Publications, entitled* The Death of Art, *to which Lang invited a number of others to respond either to my paper or to the topic.*

In each of its stages, the essay is a response to the dismal state of the artworld, for which I sought—and continue to seek—an explanation. I am increasingly persuaded by the model of art history I finally develop—it is taken a stage further in Essay IX—but it will be clear that it represents one form of the disenfranchisement of art described in Essay I. It supposes that its own philosophy is what art aims at, so that art fulfills its destiny by becoming philosophy at last. Of course art does a great deal more and less than this, which makes the death *of art an overstatement. That ours is a post-historical art, however, is a recognition deepened with each succeeding season.*

THERE ARE PHILOSOPHICAL visions of history which allow, or even demand, a speculation regarding the future of art. Such a speculation concerns the question of whether art has a future, and must be distinguished from one which merely concerns the art of the future, if we suppose art will go on and on. Indeed, the latter speculation is more difficult in a way, just because of the difficulties which go with trying to imagine what the artworks of the future will look like or how they will be appreciated. Just think how out of the question it would have been, in 1865, to predict the forms of Post-Impressionist painting, or to have anticipated, as late as 1910, that there would be, only five years in the future, a work such as Duchamp's *In Advance of the Broken Arm,* which, even when accepted as a work of art, retained its identity as a quite ordinary snow shovel. Comparable examples can be drawn from the other arts, especially as we approach our own century, when music and poetry and dance have yielded exemplars which could not have been perceived as art had anything like them appeared in earlier times, as sets of words or sounds or movements. The visionary artist Albert Robida began in 1882 the serial publication of *Le vingtième siècle.* It meant to show the world as it would be in 1952. His pictures are filled with wonders to come: *le téléphonoscope,* flying machines, television, underwater metropolises, but the pictures themselves are unmistakably of their own era, as is the way much of what they show is shown. Robida imagined there would be restaurants in the sky to which customers would come in airborne vehicles. But the boldly anticipated eating places are put together of ornamental ironworks of the sort we associate with Les Halles and the Gare St. Lazare, and look a lot like the steamboats that floated the Mississippi at that time, in proportion and in decorative fretwork. They are patronized by gentlemen in top hats and ladies in bustles, served by waiters wearing long aprons from the Belle Epoque, and they arrive in balloons Montgolfier would recognize. We may be certain that were Robida to have depicted an underwater art museum, its most advanced works would be Impressionist paintings, if Robida had eyes even for those. In 1952, the most advanced galleries were showing Pollack, De Kooning, Gottlieb, and Klein, which would have been temporally unimaginable in 1882. Nothing so much belongs to its own time as an age's glimpses into the future: Buck Rogers carries the decorative idioms of the 1930s into the twenty-first century, and *now* looks at home with Rockefeller Center and the Cord automobile; the science fiction novels of the 1950s project the sexual moralities of the Eisenhower era, along with the dry martini, into distant eons, and the technical clothing worn by its spacemen belong to that era's haberdashery. So were *we* to depict an interplanetary art gallery, it would display works which, however up to the minute they look to us, will belong to the history of art by the time there are such galleries, just as the mod clothing we put on the people we show will belong to the history of costume in no time at all. The future is a kind of mirror in which we can show only ourselves, though it seems to us a window through which we may see things to come. Leonardo's wonderful saying, that *ogni dipintore dipinge se,* implies an unintended historical limitation, as may be seen from Leonardo's own visionary drawings, so profoundly part of their own time. We may imagine *that* all sorts of things will come to be. But when we seek to *imagine* those things, they inevitably will look like things that *have* come to be, for we have only the forms we know to give them.

Even so, we may speculate historically on the future of art without committing ourselves on what the artworks of the future are to be like, if there are to be any; and it is even possible to suppose that art itself has no future, though artworks may still be produced post-historically, as it were, in the aftershock of a vanished vitality. Such indeed was a thesis of Hegel, certain of whose views have inspired the present essay, for Hegel said quite unequivocally that art as such, or at least at its highest vocation, is quite finished with as a historical moment, though he did not commit himself to the prediction that there would be no more works of art. He might have argued that, certain as he was that his astonishing thesis was true, he had nothing to say about those works to come, which might, perhaps must, be produced in ways he could not anticipate and enjoyed in ways he could not understand. I find it an extraordinary thought that the world should have gone through what one might term the Age of Art, parallel to the way in which, according to a theological speculation of the Christian theorist Joachim of Flores, the Age of the Father came to an end with the birth of His Son, and the Age of the Son with the Age of the Holy Spirit. Joachim did not claim that those whose historical fulfillment lay in the Age of the Father will become extinct or that their forms of life will abruptly disappear in the Age of the Son: they may continue to exist past the moment of their historical mission, historical fossils, so to speak, as Joachim would have supposed the Jews to be, whose time on the stage of history he believed over with. So though there will be Jews in time to come, whose forms of life may evolve in unforeseeable ways, still, their history will no longer be coincident with the history of History itself, conceived of as Joachim did, in the grandest philosophical manner.

In almost precisely this way, Hegel's thought was that for a period of time the energies of history coincided with the energies of art, but now history and art must go in different directions, and though art may continue to exist in what I have termed a post-historical fashion, its existence carries no historical significance whatever. Now such a thesis can hardly be pondered outside the framework of a philosophy of history it would be difficult to take seriously were the urgency of art's future not somehow raised from within the artworld itself, which can be seen today as having lost any historical direction, and we have to ask whether this is temporary, whether art will regain the path of history—or whether this destructured condition *is* its future: a kind of cultural entropy. So whatever comes next will not matter because the concept of art is internally exhausted. Our institutions—museums, galleries, collectors, art journals, and the like—exist against the assumption of a significant, even a brilliant, future. There is an inevitable commercial interest in what is to come now, and who are to be the important practitioners in movements next to come. It is very much in the spirit of Joachim that the English sculptor William Tucker has said, "The 60's was the age of the critic. Now it's the age of the dealer." But suppose it *has* really all come to an end, and that a point has been reached where there can be change without development, where the engines of artistic production can only combine and recombine known forms, though external pressures may favor this or that combination? Suppose it is no longer a historical possibility that art should continue to astonish us, that in this sense the Age of Art is internally worn out, and that in Hegel's stunning and melancholy phrase, a form of life has grown old?

Is it possible that the wild effervescence of the artworld in the past seven or eight decades has been a terminal fermentation of something the historical chemistry of which remains to be understood? I want to take Hegel quite seriously, and to sketch a model of the history of art in which something like it may even be said to make sense. Better to appreciate the sense it does make, I shall first sketch two rather more familiar models of art history, for the model which will finally interest me presupposes them in a striking and almost dialectical way. It is an interesting fact that though the first model has application primarily to mimetic art, to painting and sculpture and moving pictures, the second model will include them and include a great deal more of art than mimesis can easily characterize. The final model will apply to art in so comprehensive a way that the question of whether art has come to an end will have as wide a reference as the term "art" itself has, though its most dramatic reference will be to the objects purveyed in what is narrowly known as "the artworld." Indeed, part of the explanation lies in the fact that the boundaries between painting and the other arts—poetry and performance, music and dance— have become radically unstable. It is an instability induced by the factors which make my final model historically possible, and which enables the dismal question to be put. I will conclude by asking how we are to adapt to the fact that the question has an affirmative answer, that art really is over with, having become transmuted into philosophy.

Thomas Kuhn surprises us when, in the course of laying out his novel views of the history of science, he observes that painting was regarded in the nineteenth century as the progressive discipline *par excellence*: proof that progress was really possible in human affairs. The progressive model of art history derives from Vasari, who, in a phrase of Gombrich, "saw stylistic history as the gradual conquest of natural appearances." Interestingly enough, this is Gombrich's view as well, enunciated as such in his book, *The Image and the Eye*, and throughout his writings. The history of art, or at least of painting so conceived, really did come to an end, so I will begin with this familiar model.

The progress in question was largely in terms of optical duplication, in that the painter commanded increasingly refined technologies for furnishing visual experiences effectively equivalent to those furnished by actual objects and scenes. The decreasing distance between actual and pictorial optical stimulation then marks the progress in painting, and one could measure the rate of progress by the degree to which the unaided eye marks a difference. Art history demonstrated the advance, inasmuch as the unaided eye could more easily mark the differences between what Cimabue presented than what Ingres did, so art was demonstrably progressive in the way science hoped to be, granting that optics here is but a metaphor for achieving for the human mind a representation as exact as the unaided cognitions of a divine being's—though as late as Wittgenstein's *Tractatus Logico-Philosophicus* it was still a possible semantical fantasy that what Wittgenstein terms "the total natural science" should be a composite picture, logically isomorphic with the world conceived of as the sum total of facts. The history of science could then be read as the progressive shrinking of the distance between representation and reality. There was in this history a basis for the optimism that the remaining pockets of ignorance would bit by bit yield to the light, so that everything could finally be known just as, in painting, everything could finally be *shown*.

Now it is possible to give a somewhat wider conception of artistic progress than painting alone allows, by reflecting on the expansion of our representational powers brought about by the invention of moving pictures. Artists had of course long since achieved technologies for depicting things in motion: there is little doubt that Bernini's *David* depicts a young warrior in motion, propelling a stone, or that the horsemen of Leonardo are rearing, or that water in his drawings of it is surging, or that the clouds in his storm pictures are driving across the heavens. Or that Christ is raising an admonitory arm in the Arena fresco of Giotto, driving out the money lenders. Still, though we know we are looking at a moving thing, we do not see something equivalent to what moving things in fact present to the eye, for we do not see the movement. We inferred it on the basis of subtle cues implanted by the artist to motivate an inference to what correspondent objects and events would possess in real space and time. So there would have been depictions of moving things without these being *moving depictions*, and from this distinction it is possible to appreciate what moving pictures and, by retrospection, linear perspective attained to, namely the elimination, in favor of a kind of direct perception, of mediating inferences to perceptual reality facilitated by cues. Before the discovery of perspective, artists could facilitate the knowledge that we were perceiving objects receding in distance: by using occlusion, differential sizes, shadows, textural gradients, and the like. But with perspective they could actually show them as receded. One knew that the figure in the pink robe had to be closer to the window than the figure muttering at the angel, but with the technology of perspective we could more or less directly perceive this fact.

So the progress we are considering might generally be

appreciated in terms of an imperative to replace inference to
perceptual reality wherever possible with something equivalent to what perceptual reality itself would present. To be
sure, it is philosophically arguable that there is an inferential
component in even the most direct perceptual knowledge.
Even so, the inference required to move from the perception
of something equivalent to perceptual reality, to the perceptual reality itself, is distinguishable from the inference involved in the perception of reality whenever this may be
considered knowledge. Thus we may explain the posture of a
shown figure by saying it is of someone in movement. But we
see the actual movement of moving figures, and moving pictures give us something equivalent to this, where the need
for explanation is circumvented by the technologies of representation. In another kind of case, which perhaps marks a
logical limit to this progress, we always have to infer what
others are *feeling* on the basis of cues furnished in expression
and behavior. We may have to infer that what *we* are feeling is
love or anxiety—but at least we feel it, as we do not with the
love or anxiety of others. If there were something effectively
equivalent to feeling their feelings, that would be an example
of this sort of representational progress.

There are some deeply interesting aspects to this sort of
progress. For example, to the degree that we are able to
replace cues and inference with equivalences to direct perception, we approach something universal and, one may say,
nonconventional. Or at least this is so when the cues themselves are more matters of convention than we realize. Artists have worked out a code for motivating inferences to
things they could not, given the limitations of medium, directly represent. These cues are signs, the meaning of which
have independently been learned, almost the way a language
must, or at least a vocabulary. There is a marvelous art history to be written of how visual cues for smells and sounds
are planted. No group of artists has been more inventive in
this regard than comic-strip cartoonists (their ingenuity carries over into the animated cartoon), where wavy lines over

a fish mean that it stinks or a saw in a log means someone
is snoring or a series of tiny clouds mean that something
is moving. My favorite example shows the fact that a man is
turning his head by drawing his head in several positions,
united by some broken circles. *We* read this as a man turning his head, rather than a polycephalic figure of the sort
familiar in Hindu sculpture, but that is because ours is a
picture-rich culture and we have learned to do so. Show it to
members of a culture where there are other signs or who
have no pictorial need for depicting movement, and they will
not know what is going on. Or they will guess. As we have to
guess when considering pre-Columbian or Indian depictions
of this order. But when we show them movies, none of this
arises, for movies directly reach the perceptual centers involved in seeing movement, and so function at a subinferen-
tial level. Of course it took considerable time before the
movement shown was convincing: it was a matter of
"making and matching," to use Gombrich's expression, before movie-makers knew just how many frames per second
had to pass the aperture to give us an equivalent to movement as really perceived.

It is this inferential bypass to which we refer when we
speak of "fooling the senses," and there can be little question
that this was an achievement of perspective. Fooling the
senses does not of course mean fooling the viewer: our beliefs about the world form a system, and the fact that we
know we are viewing a picture neutralizes what our foolish
senses disclose. But my interest in perspective lies elsewhere
for the moment, for philosophers have at times insisted that
perspective is wholly a matter of convention and thus has
specifically to be learned, like anything symbolic—perhaps
in contrast with perceiving representations whose outlines
are congruent with the edges of things, where there is a body
of evidence which suggests that such recognition is spontaneous and perhaps wired in. It *is* true that it took a long time
for perspective to be discovered, so far as the technologies of
representation are concerned, but while artists had to learn

to show things in perspective, no one had to learn to *see* things that way. Gombrich observes that Giotto's contemporaries would have gasped at the verisimilitude of the banal depictions of bowls of cereal on our boxes of breakfast food. But their gasping would be evidence that they immediately saw how much more faithful to perceptual reality these were than Giotto's depictions, even if it took centuries for artists to learn to make convincing pictures like that. There is unfortunately not the same symmetry between recognizing and producing pictures that there is between understanding and producing sentences, which is one basis for supposing that pictorial competence differs from linguistic competence and that pictures do not constitute a language. There is a continuity between recognizing pictures and perceiving the world, but picture-making is a different sort of skill: animals are demonstrably capable of pictorial recognition, but picture-making seems exclusively a human prerogative. And its having to be learned is part of the reason that art—or at least representationalistic art—*has* a history. Our perceptual system may have evolved, but that is not the same as having a history.

What *may* be a matter of convention is the cultural decision to make pictures which look like what they are of. Other pictographic systems exist, but Vasari, and of course Gombrich, have claimed that only twice, first in ancient Greece and then in Renaissance Europe, has optical fidelity been a marked artistic aim. I think this is an underestimation. There is internal evidence that the Chinese, for example, would have used perspective if they had known about it, perhaps to their artistic detriment. For often one finds clouds and mists used to break up lines which, had they been allowed to be continuous, would have looked wrong: and a culture sensitive to optical wrongness may be described as committed to goals it has not learned to achieve. The Japanese, when they did finally see Western drawings in perspective, realized immediately what was wrong with theirs—but right or wrong from the viewpoint of perspective would make no sense if there were not an implicit pursuit of optical fidelity. The architypically Japanese artist Hokusai immediately adopted perspective when he learned of its existence—without his prints looking "western" at all. Our own optical concerns explain the presence of shadows in Western paintings and their virtual absense in many other pictorial traditions, though even when there are none, as again in Japanese art, we have to decide whether they had a different pictographic culture or simply were retarded by technological slowness in achieving solidities: that light should have a source and not be simply a diffused illumination—if indeed we can think of Japanese paintings in terms of light at all—must be connected with the same considerations under which space is regarded as defined by the eye as a source and rays which vanish at a point. I have little doubt that the oriental conception of space failed to coincide with the way orientals perceived in space, which is not, I am claiming, a matter of convention any more than the senses as a perceptual system are: we are built that way. To the degree that we regard the representation of space as merely a matter of convention, the concept of progress evaporates and the structure of art history we are discussing loses any application. I now return to that structure.

The cultural imperative to replace inference with direct perception entails a continuous effort to transform the medium of representation if the progress this imperative defines is itself to continue. I suppose we should, in fact, distinguish between the development and the transformation of the medium. Imagine a history in which we begin with the outline drawings of things, where color is implied, viewers being counted on to know what colors things of a given shape are likely to be. And then it occurs to someone to actually show those colors, so that inference is no longer required. But now, while colored shapes are a step toward verisimilitude, their relation to one another in space is a matter of inference, artists depending upon us to know what these relationships are likely to be. It then occurs to someone that variations in color and value will be seen as changes in depth, with the discovery that the sharpest values are those closest to the eye. This discovery might mark the development from icons to Cimabue and Giotto. The discovery of perspective then makes it possible to perceive as directly as we do perceive in reality how far away relative to the viewer and to one another objects are actually located. This would be an example of a development, since the medium itself is not especially altered, and we are dealing with the traditional materials of the painter, used with greater and greater effect so far as the imperative itself is concerned. But we still have to infer movement, and once it is decided that this is something we want instead to *show,* the inherent limitations of the medium become obstacles. And these limits can be overcome only by a transformation of the medium of the sort that motion-picture technology exemplifies. The change from black-and-white cinematography to color, and from single aperture spatiality to stereoscopic representation, might be regarded as the *development,* while the adjunction of sound might constitute a *transformation* of the medium. Whatever the case, increasingly complex technologies are needed for each advance at this point, and the division between development and transformation may become somewhat blurred. What I want to say is only that complexity goes with cost, and decisions have to be made as to whether we can live within the limits of our medium as it stands, or whether we are to be driven by the imperative that generates progress on to costlier and costlier mediations. Perhaps there is a parallel with the costliness of scientific advance: with each descent into the microstructure of the universe, more and more energy is demanded, and we have to make a social decision as to whether it is worth the costs to achieve the increment in cognitive control the next descent will bring. The technology is now in place for a transformation of the medium it might be well at this point to consider, namely moving holography. Thus far this has been a kind of scientific toy, though simple or still holography has been used by artists in something like

the spirit in which video has been used—as offering opportunities for artistic experiment without special reference to
the concept of progress I have been discussing. It has been
used, so to speak, for its physical possibilities, the way
Rauschenberg used the physical quality of pencil marks or
erasures.

Fixed-point perspective, as is well known, had no way
of accommodating parallax, so that if one abandons that
point in space which defines orderly recession, the scene
slumps into distortion like a failed soufflé. In the celebrated
ceiling fresco by Pozzo at St. Ignatius in Rome, in which the
saint is shown in apotheosis, the illusion of his vertical trans-
port into the heavens onto which the church opens up is
available only from a certain point below, considerately
identified by a marble disk in the floor. In fact the baroque
artist uses cloud to camouflage parallactic discrepancies to
much the same end as the Chinese used them to abort per-
spectival distortion, granting that in both cases clouds carried a spiritual and even a topographical significance—i.e.,
identifying the location as heaven or as the hills, respectively.
We have learned to live with skewed parallax in movies as
elsewhere, much, perhaps, as the Chinese viewer learned to
live with anomalous pictorial spaces or as we all learn to live
with the inconveniences of life—dust, noise, mosquitoes—in
a kind of stoicism, until it occurs to us to do something about
them, supposing something can be done. Those whom it
badly bothers have the option of finding seats in movie
houses which minimize parallactic discomfort. Holography
makes possible parrallactic conservation, with actually
rather revolutionary implications for theatrical design, in
some degree anticipated in the legitimate theater, so-called,
through theater-in-the-round. Just as this concept liberates
actors from a kind of artificial two-dimensionality imposed
by the architecture of the proscenium stage, moving holography enables cinema-in-the-round, images being liberated
from the plane of the movie screen. The images would have a
virtual three-dimensional identity, and appear, like visions,

full but impalpable, in our very midst. Priests in ancient times created illusions of gods in the uncanny space of temples by using Chinese mirrors, which enable the reflection of an actor, portraying Hercules, say, to appear detached in space, while recourse was had to clouds of incense (those ever-handy clouds!) to distract credulous celebrants from any cues to mendacity. As noted, holographic images could not be *felt*, and there would be a further question to face as to whether this was just something else to live with, or whether it was artistically worthwhile to finance research toward this further transformation of medium. Or we could retain impalpability to make an analogy to mystical vision natural, or even to provide a metaphor for art.

It is somewhat instructive to ponder this choice against a background furnished by the history of sculpture. Daedalus is legended to have confected moving dolls for the royal children of King Minos, who of course grew up to more spectacular distractions. But for the main part sculptors have preferred to allow movement to be inferred, as in the cited case of Bernini. Largely, I think, this must be because the machinery required to animate figures was unavailable, or cumbersome, or too conspicuous, and in consequence the movements too unconvincing for successful illusion: we have to remember that the ancients painted their statuary in a way doubtless too close to mortuarial cosmetics for us to be wholly comfortable. We would be even less comfortable with artificial animation: there is something evil in the idea, or at least uncanny—think of the dancing doll in *Coppélia*—and the clockwork statue of Abraham Lincoln voicing the Gettysburg Address at Disneyland is perhaps overdeterminately sickening.

Kinetic sculpture became aesthetically tolerable only when abstract, as in Calder's mobiles, where we do not have the obvious references to the real world which make the thought of moving sculpture in somewhat bad or even barbaric taste. But I have visited Hindu temples where the figures are sufficiently garishly colored that I am certain that devotees would have adored having Shiva's arms rotate like a windmill. With holography, in any case, three-dimensional nonabstract moving objects have at last the possibility of convincingness, and the two figurative practices of our tradition—picture-making and effigy-making—merge, fulfilling a fantasy of mimetic progress. And *now* I want to raise the question of whether palpability presents a further opportunity. The *Apollo Belvedere* was painted in nice pink flesh tones, I dare say, but felt cold to the touch. Marble and bronze just feel like marble and bronze, whether shaped like breasts or pectoral muscles, and no one has ever sought (before at least Duchamp) to overcome material impediments and produce effigies palpably equivalent to flesh and skin, so that Venus' emblematic breasts feel like the real thing. It would, but this is my taste, be a kind of aesthetic perversion, like fondling life-size plastic dolls of the sort manufactured for shy and hopeless men. The tackiness may diminish when movement itself becomes convincing, as in holography. But perhaps it would be imprudent to press speculation past this point, as my only aim is to illuminate some of the kinds of aesthetic and even moral considerations which enter into technical decisions in the domain of representational advance.

There is, however, one observation I cannot forebear making. Thomas Mark has maintained, I believe correctly, that there are certain musical compositions demanding high virtuosity on the part of the performer, of which it has to be said that part of what they are about is the virtuosity demanded to play them: these are what we term showpieces. But I think it very generally true that works of art often, and perhaps always in the traditional concept of the masterpieces, are about the virtuosity exacted in their execution, so that the immediate subject of the work, if it has one, is typically merely an occasion for the *real* subject, which is the display of virtuosity. Thus the brushstroke, in New York School painting, is less the subject than the occasion for displaying the real subject, which is the virtuoso action of painting. The early works which employ linear perspective use subjects which enable the perspective to be displayed, such as classical landscapes with the orderly array of columns and the recticiliar forms; wooded landscapes of the sort favored by Corot and the School of Barbizon would be useless for this purpose, and the very choice of them implies a more romantic and less regimented attitude toward space: less like a box or stage. One can sympathize with an artist like Paolo Uccello, who, since obsessed with perspective, chose unlikely subjects in order to demonstrate its power, such as battle scenes, emphasizing ranks of lances and rows of pennants, alas comically: the real battle is between subject and treatment, with Uccello as failed hero.

Now, whenever there is a technical expansion of representational possibilities, something like this internal connection between subject and technology becomes the most prominent feature of the works. When the first movies came from the studios of the Lumière brothers, the subjects chosen displayed movement for the sake of movement: a moving picture of a table full of apples would have been an idiotic choice, though it would be true that only for the first time was stillness an objective feature of the work, since only now was motion really possible. What audiences were shown was: crowds surging out of the factories, or traffic at the Place de l'Opéra, or trains, or the leafy boughs over the heads of picnickers in the Bois de Boulogne. And even today the chase as cinematic *pièce de resistance* has not cloyed. Cinerama hurled *us* through virtual space, trivially in the main, since the experiences of being on a roller coaster or a spinning airplane have deep limitations. My choice for the first holographic subject is, naturally, the Transfiguration of Christ, as described in the St. Matthew Gospel. After that I would want to see that masque which Prospero summons with a flourish of his staff out of airy nothing, for the charmed amazement of his daughter and her lover. What we will probably have, of course, will be stampeding cattle and bucking horses and cursing cattlemen. When, however, *palpability* should become a technical possibility, these could hardly be appropriate subjects: and there is a serious question of whether palpability could ever become integrated into narrative sufficiently to suppose an artistic development beyond the technical one. If films, for example, had not gone narrative, our interest in the mere display of motion would surely have paled—after all, we can see the real thing any time we want. And I think it generally the case that unless mimesis becomes transformed into diegesis, or narative, an artform dies of diminishing excitement.

Whatever the case, it has always been possible to imagine, at least grossly, the future of art construed in terms of representational progress. One knew in principle what the agenda was, and hence what progress would have to be if there was to be progress. Visionaries could say such things as "Someday pictures will move," without knowing how it was to be achieved, just as not long ago they could say, "Someday men will walk on the moon," without knowing, again, quite how *this* was to be achieved. But then, and this has been the main reason for canvassing this entire theory, it would be possible to speak of the end of art, at least as a progressive discipline. When, for every perceptual range R, an equivalent could be technically generated, then art would be over with, just as science would be over with when, as was thought to be a genuine possibility in the nineteenth century, everything was known. In the nineteenth century, for example, it was believed that logic was a finished science, and even that physics was, with a few nagging details to mop up. But there is no internal reason for us to think that science, or art, has be be endless, and so there was always a question that would have to be faced, as to what post-progressive life would be like. To be sure, we have more or less abandoned this model in art, since the production of perceptual equivalence no longer much dazzles us, and in any case there are certain definite limits set when narrativization becomes an artistic fact. Even so, as we shall see, the model has an oblique pertinence even today.

Before coming to that, however, I want to raise a philosophical point. So long as the philosophy of art was articulated in terms of success or failure in technologies of perceptual equivalence, it would have been difficult to get an interestingly general definition of art. Aristotle widened the notion of imitation to include the imitation of an action, in order to bring narrative drama into the scope of that concept, but at that point the theory of mimesis parts company with the concept of perceptual equivalences, since it is far from plain that drama presents us with merely perceptual equivalences to what a sort of eyewitness to the action would perceive. And while this is, in the case of dramatic presentations, a mistakenly entertainable ideal, it is not so at all when we consider *fiction* as the description of an action. And when we think of description as against mimesis, we may immediately notice that it is not at all clear that there is any room for the concept of progress or of technological transformations at all. Let me explain this.

Thinkers have, from Lao Tzu to the present, lamented or celebrated the inadequacies of language. It is felt that there are descriptive limits, and then important things beyond these limits which language cannot express. But to the degree that this is true, no expansion of representational possibilities, say by introducing new terms into the language, will remedy the situation, largely because the complaint is against descriptivity itself, which simply is too distant from reality to give us the experience reality itself affords. And it is a mark of the natural languages that whatever can be said in one can be said in any (and what *cannot* be said in one cannot be said in any), allowing always for differences of felicity and degrees of roundaboutness. So there cannot ever have been a technological problem of expanding the descriptive resources of the natural languages: they are equivalently universal.

I do not mean to imply that there are no limits to language, but only that whatever they are, nothing is going to count as progress toward their overcoming, since this would still be within language as a representational system. So there is no logical room for the concept of progress. At no point in the history of literature, for example, would visionaries have been able to prophesy that someday men will be able to say certain things—in part perhaps because in saying what men will be able to say, it is *already* said. Of course someone might have been able to say that someday men will be able to talk about things then forbidden, sex perhaps, or be able to use language to criticize institutions which they are not able to do now. But this would be a matter of moral progress, or political progress, if it is that, and would have as much application to pictures as to words. Whatever the value of doing so, we can today see things in movies it would have been unthinkable to show a generation ago—the star's breasts, say. But this is not *technological* advance.

The linear or progressive model of the history of art thus finds its best examples in painting and sculpture, then in movies and talkies and, if you wish, feelies. There has never been a problem of *describing* motion, or depth, or for that matter palpability. "Her soft and yielding flesh" describes a perceptual experience for which there is no mimetic equivalent. Our next model will make a more general definition possible, since it is not thwarted by the differences between words and pictures. But then it eliminates those factors from the essence of art which made it possible to think of art as a progressive discipline.

I like to surmise that a confirmation of my historical thesis—that the task of art to produce equivalences to perceptual experiences passed, in the late nineteenth and early twentieth centuries, from the activities of painting and sculpture to those of cinematography—in the fact that painters and sculptors began conspicuously to abandon this goal at just about the same time that all the basic strategies for narrative cinema were in place. By about 1905, almost every cinematic strategy since employed had been discovered, and it was just about then that painters and sculptors began asking, if only through their actions, the question of what could be left for *them* to do, now that the torch had, as it were, been taken up by other technologies. I suppose that the history of artistic progress could be run backward: we can imagine the projected end state as having been achieved, but now it seems a good idea, for whatever reason, to replace perceptual equivalences with cues to inference—perhaps because a greater value gets put on inference (= Reason) than on perception. Bit by bit cinematography gets replaced with the cues to kinematic motion of the sort we find in Rosa Bonheur or Rodin, and so on, until, I suppose, perceptual equivalence disappears from art altogether and we get an art of pure descriptivity, where words replace perceptual stimuli. And who knows, this may seem too closely tied to experience and the next move might be music. But given the way progress itself *was* conceived, about 1905 it appeared that painters and sculptors could only justify their activities by redefining art in ways which had to be shocking indeed to those who continued to judge painting and sculpture by the criteria of the progressive paradigm, not realizing that a transformation in technology now made practices appropriate to those critera more and more archaic.

The Fauves are good examples. Consider the portrait by Matisse of his wife done in 1906, in which Madame Matisse is shown with a green stripe down her nose (indeed, the title of the painting is *The Green Stripe*). Chiang Yee told me of a painting done by a Jesuit artist of a Chinese emperor's favorite concubine, which shocked her, since she knew her face was not half black and *he* used shadows. Instruction on how the world really looks would have made her recognize that *she* really looked the way he had shown her, given the realities of light and shade. But nothing of that sort is going to redeem Matisse's painting for the history of perceptual equivalences, not even if there happened to be a greenish shadow along his subject's nose—for it would not have been *that* particular green. Nor were ladies at that time using nose shadow as those of our time use eye shadow. Nor was she

suffering nasal gangrene. So one could only conclude (as
people did) that Matisse had forgotten how to paint, had
remembered how to paint but had gone crazy, was sane but
was perverting his skills to the end of shocking the bour-
geoisie, or trying to put something over on the collectors,
critics, and curators (who are the three C's of the artworld).

These would have been standard rationalizations of objects, beginning to appear in epidemic quantity just then,
which were unquestionably *paintings*, but which fell short by
so considerable a degree of perceptual equivalence to anything in either the real world or the artworld, that some
explanation of their existence seemed imperative. Until, that
is, it began to be grasped that only relative to a theory which
may have been put to a challenge was there any discrepancy
at all, and that if there was one, well, it might be the fault
of the theory. In science, ideally at least, we don't blame the
world when our theories don't work—we change the theories
until they do work. And so it was with Post-Impressionist
painting. It became increasingly clear that a new theory was
urgently required, that the artists were not failing to yield up
perceptual equivalences but were after something not to be
understood in those terms primarily or at all. It is to the
credit of aesthetics that its practitioners responded to this
with theories which, however inadequate, recognized the
need, and a good example of at least a suitable theory was
that painters were not so much representing as expressing.
Croce's *Estetica come scienza dell'espressione* appeared in 1902.
Suppose then that *The Green Stripe* tries to get us to see how
Matisse felt about the subject shown, his own wife, calling
for a complex act of interpretation on the part of the viewer.

This account is remarkable for the fact that it incorporates the theory of perceptual equivalences in the sense that
it presupposes the discrepancies, which it then explains as
due to feelings. It acknowledges, as it were, the intensional
character of emotional states, that feelings are *about*, or
toward, some object or state of affairs; and since Croce supposes art to be a kind of language, and language a form of

communication, the communication of feeling will succeed
to just the extent that the work can show what object it is
toward which the feeling is expressed—e.g., the artist's wife.
Then the discrepancies between the way this object is in fact
shown and the way it would be shown were mere perceptual
equivalence aimed at, no longer marks a distance to be covered by the progress of art or by the artist's mastery of illu-
sionist technique, but rather consists in the externalization or
objectification of the artist's feelings toward what he shows.
The feeling is then communicated to the viewer to just the
degree that the viewer can infer it on the basis of the discrepancies. Indeed, the viewer must generate some hypothesis to
the effect that the object is shown the way it is because the
artist feels about the object the way he does. Thus De Kooning paints a woman as the locus of slashes, El Greco paints
saints as stretched verticalities, Giacometti molds figures as
impossibly emaciated, not for optical reasons nor because
there really are women, saints, or persons like these, but
because the artists respectively reveal feelings of ag-
gressiveness, spiritual longing, or compassion. It would be
very difficult to suppose De Kooning is expressing compassion, let alone spirituality, or that El Greco is expressing aggression. But of course the ascription of feelings is always
epistemologically delicate.

It becomes particularly delicate when the theory recommends the view that the object represented by the work becomes the occasion for expressing something about it, and
we then begin to reconstitute the history of art along these
new lines. For we now have to decide to what degree the
discrepancies with an ideal perceptual equivalence are a
matter of technical shortfall, and to what degree a matter of
expression. Obviously we are not to read all discrepancies as
expressive, for then the concept of progress no longer applies: we must assume that in a great many cases an artist
would eliminate discrepancies if he but knew how. Even so,
certain discrepancies which would be laughable from the
point of view of representation become artistically funda-

mental from that of expression. At the time of the Fauves, the deviations emphasized by apologists of the new art and subscribers to the new theory were made acceptable by pointing to the fact that the artist after all could *draw*: one pointed in evidence to Matisse's academic exercises, or to Picasso's amazing canvases of his sixteenth year. But these anxious questions lost their force after a time as expression seemed more and more to carry the definitional properties of art. Objects became less and less recognizable and finally disappeared altogether in Abstract Expressionism, which of course meant that interpretation of purely expressionist work required reference to objectless feelings: joy, depression, generalized excitement, etc. What was interesting was the fact that since there could be paintings which were purely expressive and hence not explicitly representational at all, representationality must disappear from the definition of art. But even *more* interesting from our perspective is the fact that the *history* of art acquires a totally different structure.

It does so because there is no longer any reason to think of art as having a progressive history: there simply is not the possibility of a developmental sequence with the concept of expression as there is with the concept of mimetic representation. There is not because there is no mediating technology of expression. I do not mean to imply that novel technologies of representation may not admit novel modes of expression: beyond question there are expressive possibilities in cinema that simply had no parallel in the kind of art cinema transformed. But these new possibilities would not constitute a progressive development—viz., there would be no basis for saying that we now can express what we could express badly or not at all before, as we could say that we now can show things we could only show badly or not at all before. So the history of art has no future of the sort that can be extrapolated as it can against the paradigm of progress: it sunders into a sequence of individual acts, one after another. Of course there may be feelings one dare not express at a given time but which in time one can express, but the raising or lowering of the thresholds of expressive inhibition belong to the history of morality. And of course there may be a history of *learning* to express feelings, as through a kind of therapy, but then this would belong to the general history of freedom, with no particular application to art. Heidegger has said that not one step has been taken since Aristotle's *Rhetoric* in the philosophical analysis of feelings—but this surely is because the range of human feelings can be very little different from what it was in ancient times. There may be new objects for these feelings, even new ways of expressing them—but once more this is not a development history.

There is a further point. Once art becomes construed as expression, the work of art must send us ultimately to the state of mind of its maker, if we are to interpret it. Realistically speaking, artists of a given period share a certain expressive vocabulary, which is why, right or wrong, my casual interpretations of De Kooning, El Greco, and Giacometti seem at least natural. Even so, this seems to me a quite external fact, not at all necessary to the concept of expression, and conceivably each artist could express himself in his own way, so that one vocabulary, as it were, would be incommensurable with another, which makes possible a radically discontinuous view of the history of art, in which one style of art follows another, as in an archipelago, and we might in principle imagine any sequence we choose. In any case we must understand each work, each corpus, in the terms that define that particular artist we are studying, and what is true of De Kooning need have nothing to do with what is true of anyone else. The concept of expression makes such a view possible, relativizing art, as it does, to individual artists. The history of art is just the lives of the artists, one after another.

It is striking that the history of science is thought of somewhat along these lines today—not, as in the optimism of the nineteenth century, as a linear, inevitable progression toward an end state of total cognitive representation, but as a discontinuous sequence of phases between which there is a radical incommensurability. It is almost as though the semantics of scientific terms were like the semantics of terms like "pain," where each user is referring to something different and speaking in a private idiom—so that to the degree that we understand one another at all, we do so on our own terms. Thus "mass" means something different in each phase of science, in part because it is redefined with each theory that employs it, so that synonymy between theory and theory is ruled out. But even if we stop short of this extreme lexical radicalism, the mere structure of history might insure some degree of incommensurability. Imagine the history of art reversed, so that it begins with Picasso and Matisse, passes through Impressionism and the Baroque, suffers a decline with Giotto, only to reach its pinnacle with the original of the *Apollo Belvedere*, beyond which it would be impossible to imagine a further advance. Strictly speaking, the works in question *could* have been produced in that order. But they could not have the interpretation, nor hence the structure, we perceive them as having under the present chronology. Picasso, only for example, is constantly referring to the history of art he systematically deconstructs, and so presupposes those past works. And something of the same sort is true of science. Even if scientists are not as conscious of their history as artists are, in truth there are intertheoretic references which assure a degree of incommensurability, if only because we know Galileo and he could not have known us, and to the degree that our uses refer to his, the terms we use cannot have the same meanings his did. So there is an important respect in which we *have* to understand the past in our *own* terms, and there can in consequence be no uniform usage from phase to phase.

There have been philosophies of history which have made these incommensurabilities central, if not for precisely the reasons I have sketched. I am thinking just now of Spengler, who dissolved what had been assumed to be the linear history of the West into three distinct and self-contained historical periods, Classical, Magian, and Faustian, each with its own vocabulary of cultural forms, between which no commensurability of meaning could be assumed. The classical temple, the domed basilica, the vaulted cathedral are less three moments in a linear history than three distinct expressions in the medium of architecture of distinct underlying cultural spirits. In some absolute sense the three periods succeed one another, but only in the way in which one generation succeeds another, with the specific analogy to be drawn that each generation reaches and expresses its maturity in its own way. Each of them defines a different world, and it is the worlds that are incommensurable. Spengler's book was notoriously titled *The Decline of the West,* and it was reckoned exceedingly pessimistic when it first appeared, in part because of the biological metaphors Spengler employed, which required each of his civilizations to go through its own cycle of youth, maturity, decline, and death. So the future of *our* art is very dim, if we accept his premises, but—and how optimistic he after all was—a new cycle will begin, with its own peaks, and we can no more imagine it than *we* could have been imagined from an earlier cycle. So *art* will have a future, it is only that *our* art will not. *Ours* is a form of life that has grown old. So you could look on Spengler as saying something dark or something bright, depending upon how you feel about your own culture within the framework of the severe relativism it, as indeed all the views I have been discussing in this section, presupposes.

And the reason I am stressing this relativism here is that the question I began with, whether art has a future, clearly is antirelativistic in that it really does presuppose a linear history in some sense. This has an absolutely profound philosophical implication, in that it requires an internal connection between the way we define art and the way we think of the history of art. Only, for instance, if we first think of art as representation can we then think of art as having the sort of history which fulfills the progressive model. If, on the other hand, we think of art as simply being expression, or the communication of feelings, as Croce did, well, it just can't have a history of that sort and the question of the end of art can have no application, just because the concept of expression goes with that sort of incommensurability in which one thing just comes after another thing. So that even if it is a fact that artists express feelings, well, this is only a fact, and cannot be the essence of art *if* art has the kind of history within which the question of its coming to an end makes sense. That art is the business of perceptual equivalence is consistent with its having that sort of history, but then, as we saw, it is insufficiently general as a definition of art. So what emerges from this dialectic is that if we are to think of art as having an end, we need a conception of art history which is linear, but a theory of art which is general enough to include representations other than the sort illusionistic painting exemplifies best: literary representations, for example, and even music.

Now Hegel's theory meets all these demands. His thought requires that there be genuine historical continuity, and indeed a kind of progress. The progress in question is not that of an increasingly refined technology of perceptual equivalence. Rather, there is a kind of *cognitive* progress, where it is understood that art progressively approaches that kind of cognition. When the cognition is achieved, there really is no longer any point to or need for art. Art is a transitional stage in the coming of a certain kind of knowledge. The question then is what sort of cognition this can be, and the answer, disappointing as it must sound at first, is the knowledge of what art is. Just as we saw is required, there is an internal connection between the nature and the history of art. History ends with the advent of self-consciousness, or better, self-knowledge. I suppose in a way our personal histories have that structure, or at least our educational histories do, in that they end with maturity, where maturity is understood as knowing—and accepting—what or even who we are. Art ends with the advent of its own philosophy. I shall now tell this last story by returning to the history of past perceptual art.

The success of the Expression Theory of art is also the

failure of the Expression Theory of art. Its success consisted in the fact that it was able to explain all of art in a uniform way—i.e., as the expression of feelings. Its failure consisted in the fact that it has only one way of explaining all of art. When discontinuities first appeared as puzzling phenomena in the progressive history of representation, it was a genuine insight that perhaps artists were trying to express rather than primarily to represent. But after about 1906, the history of art simply seemed to be the history of discontinuities. To be sure, this could be accommodated to the theory. Each of us has his or her own feelings, so it is to be expected that these will be expressed in individual ways, and even in incommensurable ways. Most of us, of course, express our feelings in very similar ways, and there are forms of expression which must in fact be understood in evolutionary, not to say physiological, terms: we are built to express feelings in ways we all recognize. But then the theory is that these are artists and artists are defined in part through the uniqueness of their feelings. The artist is different from the rest of us. But the trouble with this plausible if romantic account lay in the fact that each new movement, from Fauvism down, let alone the Post-Impressionism from which that derived, seemed to require some kind of *theoretical* understanding to which the language and the psychology of emotions seemed less and less adequate.

Just think of the dazzling succession of art movements in our century: Fauvism, the Cubisms, Futurism, Vorticism, Synchronism, Abstractionism, Surrealism, Dada, Expressionism, Abstract Expressionism, Pop, Op, Minimalism, Post-Minimalism, Conceptualism, Photorealism, Abstract Realism, Neo-Expressionism—simply to list some of the more familiar ones. Fauvism lasted about two years, and there was a time when a whole period of art history seemed destined to endure about five months, or half a season. Creativity at that time seemed more to consist in making a period than in making a work. The imperatives of art were virtually historical imperatives—Make an art-historical pe-

riod!—and success consisted in producing an accepted inno-
vation. If you were successful, you had the monopoly on
producing works no one else could, since no one else had
made the period with which you and perhaps a few collaborators were from now on to be identified. With this went a
certain financial security, inasmuch as museums, wedded to
historical structure and the kind of completeness which went
with having examples from each period, would want an example from you if you were a suitable period. As innovative
an artist as De Kooning was never especially allowed to
evolve, and De Chirico, who understood these mechanisms
exactly, painted de chiricos throughout his life, since that's
what the market wanted. Who would want a Utrillo that
looked like Mondrian, or a Marie Laurencin that looked like
Grace Hartigan, or a Modigliani like Franz Kline? And each
period required a certain amount of quite complex theory in
order that the often very minimal objects could be transacted
onto the plane of art. In the face of this deep interplay between historical location and theoretical enfranchisement,
the appeal to feeling and expression seemed just less and less
convincing. Even today we hardly know what Cubism was
really about, but I am certain that there is a great deal more
to it than Braque and Picasso ventilating their surprisingly
congruent feelings toward guitars.

The Expression Theory, while too thin by far to account
for this rich profusion of artistic styles and genres, has nevertheless the great merit of having approached works of art
as constituting a natural kind, surface variations notwithstanding, and to have responded in the spirit of science to
what has been a brooding question since Plato—namely,
What is Art? The question became urgent in the twentieth
century, when the received model collapsed, though that
was not even a good model when no one could tell that it
was not. But the inadequacy of the theory became year by
year—or, if I may, period by period—more apparent as each
movement raised the question afresh, offering itself as a possible final answer. The question indeed accompanied each

new artform as the Cogito, according to a great thesis of
Kant's, accompanies each judgment, as though each judgment raises about itself the question of What is Thought?
And it began to seem as though the whole main point of art
in our century was to pursue the question of its own identity
while rejecting all available answers as insufficiently general.
It was as though, to paraphrase a famous formula of Kant,
art were something conceptuable without satisfying any specific concept.

It is this way of looking at things which suggests another
model of art history altogether, a model narratively exemplified by the *Bildungsroman*, the novel of self-education
which climaxes in the self's recognition of the self. This is a
genre recently and, I think, not inappropriately to be mainly
found in feminist literature, where the question the heroine
raises, for reader and for herself, is at once who is she and
what is it to be a woman. The great philosophical work
which has this form is Hegel's astonishing *Phenomenology of
Spirit*, a work whose hero is the spirit of the world—whom
Hegel names *Geist*—the stages of whose development toward
self-knowledge, and toward self-realization through self-
knowledge, Hegel traces dialectically. Art is one of these
stages—indeed, one of the nearly final stages of spirit's return to spirit through spirit—but it is a stage which must be
gone through in the painful ascent toward the final redeeming cognition.

The culmination of Geist's quest and destiny is, as it
happens, philosophy, according to Hegel's scheme, largely
because philosophy is essentially reflexive, in the sense that
the question of what it is is part of what it is, its own nature
being one of its major problems. Indeed, the history of philosophy may be read as the story of philosophy's mistaken
identities, and of its failures in seeing through and to itself. It
is possible to read Hegel as claiming that art's philosophical
history consists in its being absorbed ultimately into its own
philosophy, demonstrating then that self-theoretization is a
genuine possibility and guarantee that there is something

whose identity consists in self-understanding. So the great drama of history, which in Hegel is a divine comedy of the mind, can end in a moment of final self-enlightenment, where the enlightenment consists in itself. The historical importance of art then lies in the fact that it makes philosophy of art possible and important. Now if we look at the art of our recent past in these terms, grandiose as they are, what we see is something which depends more and more upon theory for its existence as art, so that theory is not something external to a world it seeks to understand, so that in understanding its object it has to understand itself. But there is another feature exhibited by these late productions which is that the objects approach zero as their theory approaches infinity, so that virtually all there is at the end *is* theory, art having finally become vaporized in a dazzle of pure thought about itself, and remaining, as it were, solely as the object of its own theoretical consciousness.

If something like this view has the remotest chance of being plausible, it is possible to suppose that art had come to an end. Of course, there will go on being art-making. But art-makers, living in what I like to call the post-historical period of art, will bring into existence works which lack the historical importance or meaning we have for a very long time come to expect. The historical stage of art is done with when it is known what art is and means. The artists have made the way open for philosophy, and the moment has arrived at which the task must be transferred finally into the hands of philosophers. Let me conclude by spelling this out in a way which might make it acceptable.

"The end of history" is a phrase which carries ominous overtones at a time when we hold it in our power to end everything, to expel mankind explosively from being. Apocalypse has always been a possible vision, but has seldom seemed so close to actuality as it is today. When there is nothing left to make history—i.e., no more human beings—

there will be no more history. But the great meta-historians of the nineteenth century, with their essentially religious readings of history, had rather something more benign in mind, even if, in the case of Karl Marx, violence was to be the engine of this benign culmination. For these thinkers, history was some kind of necessary agony through which the end of history was somehow to be earned, and the end of history then meant the end of that agony. History comes to an end, but not mankind—as the story comes to an end, but not the characters, who live on, happily ever after, doing whatever they do in their post-narrational insignificance. Whatever they do and whatever now happens to them is not part of the story lived through them, as though they were the vehicle and it the subject.

Here is a pertinent summation by that profound and influential commentator on Hegel, Alexandre Kojève:

In point of fact, the end of human time, or History—that is, the definitive annihilation of Man, properly speaking, or of the free and historical individual—means quite simply the cessation of action in the full sense of the term. Practically, this means the disappearance of wars and bloodly revolutions. And also the disappearance of Philosophy. For since Man no longer changes essentially, there is no reason to change the (true) principles which are at the basis of his understanding of the world and himself. But all the rest can be preserved indefinitely: art, love, play, etc.: in short, everything that makes man *happy*.

And Marx, in a famous passage upon which there can be little doubt that Kojève based his, describes the life of man when all the contradictions that define history, and which are expressed socially as the class wars so ominously specified in *The Communist Manifesto*, have worked themselves out through the agony of history, so that society is now classless and there is nothing left to generate more history, and man is deposited on the promised shores of utopia, a paradise of nonalienation and nonspecialization. There, Marx tells us, I can be a hunter in the morning and a fisher in the afternoon and a critical critic in the evening. Post-historical life, for Hegel as for Marx, will have the form of a kind of philosophical *Club mediterranée*, or what used to be known as heaven, where there is nothing left for us to do but—in the phrase of our adolescents—hang out. Or, to take another image, this time from Plato, where, at the end of his *Republic*, he depicts a choosing situation, in which men, purged in the afterlife and ready to reenter the world, have arrayed before them the variety of lives from which they may pick one: and the canny Odysseus chooses a life of quiet obscurity, the sort of life most people live most of the time, the simple dumb existence of the sitcom, village life, domestic life, the kind of life lamented, in a painful episode, by Achilles in the underworld. Only, in Marx and in Hegel, there is no history to rumble beyond the distant horizons. The storms have abated forever. And now we can do what we like, heeding that imperative that is no imperative at all: *Fay çe que voudras*—"Do whatever you want."

The End of History coincides, and is indeed identical, with what Hegel speaks of as the advent of Absolute Knowledge. Knowledge is absolute when there is no gap between knowledge and its object, or knowledge is its own object, hence subject and object at once. The closing paragraph of the *Phenomenology* suitably characterizes the philosophical closure of the subject it treats of, by saying that it "consists in perfectly knowing itself, in knowing what it is." Nothing is now outside knowledge, nor opaque to the light of cognitive intuition. Such a conception of knowledge is, I believe, fatally flawed. But if anything comes close to exemplifying it, art in our times does—for the object in which the artwork consists is so irradiated by theoretical consciousness that the division between object and subject is all but overcome, and it little matters whether art is philosophy in action or philosophy is art in thought. "It is no doubt the case," Hegel writes in his *Philosophy of the Fine Arts*, "that art can be utilized as a mere pastime and entertainment, either in the embellishment of our surroundings, the imprinting of a life-enhancing surface to the external conditions of our life, or the emphasis placed by decoration on other subjects." Some such function must be what Kojève has in mind when he speaks of art as among the things that will make men happy in the post-historical time. It is a kind of play. But this kind of art, Hegel contends, is not really free, "since subservient to other objects." Art is truly free, he goes on to say, only when "it has established itself in a sphere it shares with religion and philosophy, becoming thereby one mode more and form through which . . . the spiritual truths of widest range are brought home to consciousness." All this and, being Hegel, a good bit more having been said, he concludes, dismally or not I leave it to the reader to determine, "Art is and remains for us a thing of the past." And: "On the side of its highest possibilities [art] has lost its genuine truth and life, and is rather transported to our world of *ideas* than is able to maintain its former necessity and its superior place in reality." So a "science of art," or *Kunstwissenschaft*—by which certainly Hegel meant nothing remotely like art history as practiced as an academic discipline today, but rather instead a sort of cultural philosophy of the sort he himself was working out— a "science of art is a far more urgent necessity in our own times than in times in which art sufficed by itself alone to give full satisfaction." And further on in this utterly amazing passage he says, "We are invited by art to contemplate it reflectively . . . in order to ascertain scientifically its nature." And this is hardly something art history as we know it attempts to do, though I am certain that the present rather anemic discipline grew out of something as robust in its conception as Hegel meant for it to be. But it is also possible that art history has the form we know because art as we knew it is finished.

Well.

As Marx might say, you can be an abstractionist in the morning, a photorealist in the afternoon, a minimal minimalist in the evening. Or you can cut out paper dolls or do what you damned please. The age of pluralism is upon us. It does not matter any longer what you do, which is what pluralism means. When one direction is as good as another direction, there is no concept of direction any longer to apply. Decoration, self-expression, entertainment are, of course, abiding human needs. There will always be a service for art to perform, if artists are content with that. Freedom ends in its own fulfillment. A subservient art has always been with us. The institutions of the artworld—galleries, collectors, exhibitions, journalism—which are predicated upon history and hence marking what is new, will bit by bit wither away. How happy happiness will make us is difficult to foretell, but just think of the difference the rage for gourmet cooking has made in common American life. On the other hand, it has been an immense privilege to have lived in history.

VI.

Art and Disturbation

Noel Carroll invited my participation in a symposium on nonstandard genres of art, held at the avant-garde gallery The Kitchen, in 1984. The sort of genre he had in mind would be exemplified by video, opera, and performance art. The latter had intrigued me as it straddles painting and theater, and hence is held in galleries but for participant audiences. I offer the essay as a case study of one effort to meet the crisis to which modernism is in general a response, but one which goes backward, as it were to the cloudiest beginnings of art, rather than forward to its transfiguration into philosophy. So this essay carries forward the historical speculations of "The End of Art," and prepares the way for those in "Art, Evolution, and the Consciousness of History." This essay appeared in Formations, *Winter 1985.*

IN THE LATE nineteenth century, the task of redefining the art of painting from within became a matter of such urgency as virtually to constitute the subject of painting, if not indeed of art as such, throughout the present century. In "The End of Art" I tendered a reading of the history of painting from the Renaissance until that crucial moment as very largely addressed to the technology of illusion, of producing perceptual equivalences to what the natural appearances of things would induce in a spectator—even the Impressionists continued this collective project—and the crisis of redefinition I then attribute to the recognition that a novel technology was in place for achieving this over a far wider range of appearances than painting could hope to conquer. I had in mind moving pictures, pictures which directly represent motion by means of moving images, thus facilitating narrative representation in a way closed off to painting. Painting was therefore required to redefine itself or collapse into a secondary activity, purveying decorations and illustrations, but no longer in position to transform consciousness in a manner taken for granted by the Parisian populace that demanded that David depict the death of Marat. Painting responded to this challenge so heroically as to set up severe perturbations along boundary lines that had been stable for so long a time as to have been accepted as natural frontiers. I refer first to the various boundary lines which separated one art from another—painting from poetry, drama from dance, music from sculpture—and then the boundaries which sectioned art off from philosophy in one direction and from life in the other. So the history of art in the twentieth century has been the history of transformations and revolutionizations of the concept of art in a kind of conceptual warfare so intense and unresolved that the face of high culture is a kind of no-man's land, with the possibility that art today is just destabilization, owing its continued existence to the memory of boundaries no one can any longer respect.

I suppose the arts of collage and assemblage, of mobile sculpture and concrete poetry, exemplify the sorts of internal realignments that might be made without calling too sharply into question the two heavier boundaries between art and its own philosophy, and between art and life, that philosophy more or less assumed indelible. Of these I have naturally been most concerned with the first, since any instability at its boundary must induce a rethinking of philosophy from within, for if it cannot cleanly distinguish itself from one of its subjects, it scarcely finally knows what it itself is. Indeed, so entwined are the histories of philosophy and art that the self-definition of philosophy is hostage to the philosophy of art, as I have tried to show in these pages. In this essay, however, I mean to concern myself with that extraordinary profusion of artforms that have grown up like shantytowns at the edges of what used to be thought of as the limits of art: artforms which seem on the surface to be endeavoring to drive these limits back, to colonize, as it were, the west bank of life by art—artforms marked by a curious ephemerality and indefinition, and which I shall designate as the arts of disturbation.

The term is meant, of course, to allude to its natural rhyme in English, since masturbation is an activity which straddles a similar boundary, in that certain images and fantasies have outward effects—mere charged images climax in real orgasms, and induce a real reduction of tension. And in a way this models what the art of disturbation seeks to achieve, to produce an existential spasm through the intervention of images into life. But the term is also meant to retain the connotations of disturbance, for these various arts, often in consequence of their improvisational and shabby execution, carry a certain threat, promise a certain danger even, compromise reality in a way the more entrenched arts and their descendants have lost the power to achieve. Perhaps it is for this reason that the spontaneous response to disturbational art is to disarm it by cooptation, incorporating it instantaneously into the cool institutions of the artworld where it will be rendered harmless and distant from forms of life it meant to explode. This makes the museum and the avant-garde theater outposts of civilization, a factor to keep in mind when one accuses them of trendiness.

Let me begin, in any case, by drawing a contrast between disturbational art and art which is disturbing in the traditional sense in which it was always open to art to be— namely, through representing disturbing things even in disturbing ways. There is, for example, today hardly a more disturbing set of images than those to be found in the late paintings of Leon Golub, whose work in a Whitney Biennial made the rest of what appeared in those galleries look like so many toys. These are large, banner-like expanses of unmounted canvas on which Golub depicts terrorists and torturers, at work on their bound and hooded victims or at play with girlfriends whose reduction to sexual objecthood matches the reduction to mere objects of the persons in their power. Golub puts the viewer in the same space with these monsters, by entering it himself, addressing them from the posture of a photographer who asks them to smile, to look nice, to say "Cheese"—and they turn to the camera and strike a pose, clown, horse around, perhaps ask for a copy to send home, as the flashgun lights up the agony of the airless garages and warehouses in which they carry out their mindless inhumanities. The inhumanity is utterly unredeemed, by contrast with depictions of martyrdoms in Christian art where the suffering is made vivid because it has a point in Christian ethics and is made disturbing in order to enlist the compassion of the viewer for his or her own salvation. No doubt this is necessary in view of the fact that the crucifixions, which make up so much of the substance of Western art, shrink finally into so many decorations. The political realities that Golub's paintings emblemize are certainly unredeemed by any of the purposes politics is meant to serve, but my concern is only to stress that they are disturbing in that what they show is disturbing, as is the way it is shown—but no more disturbing than *King Lear* is or *Oedipus Rex*: and meanwhile we view them in a polished gallery, surrounded by the swank eastside artfolk, and the fact that these ghastly visions can be contained carries a compensatory comfort matched, I suppose, by the utter security a child has as it listens to its mother tell the familiar tales of terrible things the child has no way of knowing are not true, lying in its warm bed with stuffed bears and cocoa near at hand: the horror of the narrated happening even increases the security it feels, which may explain the eternal popularity of fairy tales. And perhaps of horror movies we go to because we need the assurances about our own lives they provide. We

turn from Golub in just this way and just because his works
are paintings, framed by the amenities of the artworld and
set off by a life whose basic pleasantness they underscore: we
may remind ourselves to send a check to Amnesty Interna-
tional as we turn to the confections of Nancy Graves or the
muddled constructions of Jonathan Borofsky. In its time-
honored way, even disturbing art but puts disturbing realities
at a distance, and in so doing may after all discharge one of
the functions for which art was invented. This is not what I
mean by disturbational art intended, by exact contrast, to
subvert that function. Golub is constrained by the conventions of art to have his intended screams sweetened into
arias.

So it is disturbation when the insulating boundaries between art and life are breached in some way the mere representation of disturbing things cannot achieve just because
they are representations and responded to as such. It is for
this reason that reality must in some way then be an actual
component of disturbational art, and usually reality of a kind
itself disturbing: obscenity, frontal nudity, blood, excrement,
mutilation, real danger, actual pain, possible death. And
these as components in the art, not simply collateral with its
production or appreciation—as when the scaffolding holding the plasterers collapses, or the painter falls off the ladder,
or an artist dies of blood poisoning, or a passerby dies from a
fallen piece of entablature.

I have always drawn a certain philosophical inspiration
from the work of Jasper Johns, especially from his exploita-
tions of a class of images which instantly become examples
of what they represent, so that with them the line between
reality and representation is dissolved. A picture of a numeral, for instance, *is* a numeral, as an image of a map is a
map. You cannot represent the reality, accordingly, without
reproducing it. These cases—flags, letters, emblems are further examples—seem exactly to be what Plato had in mind
by mimetic representations as a class: the words an actor

speaks, for example, represent but also consist of the very words the character speaks, so dialogue represents by presentations. Since the words spoken by the actor are real words, the dialogue of the play puts on the stage a real conversation, and Plato thought mimesis a very dangerous form of representation, since the actors were to be the guardians whose education he was designing, and he worried about the consequences of putting real words in their mouths unless they were good words spoken by good characters. Johns employs some of the mechanisms of disturbational art as high art, chiefly because the reality he deals with is not disturbing reality of the sort Plato, for example, was anxious to exclude from dramatic representation.

Now something like the platonic superstition remains, or remained until quite recently, in effect with regard to obscenities. It was widely accepted that one could not mention an obscenity without through that very act *using* the obscenity: obscenity was a kind of solvent that ate through the device even of quotation or display, so that the effort at mere imitation of the obscene utterance was doomed: there was no allowed distance of the sort that had long since insinuated itself in dramatic representation, separating the words the actor spoke from those the character spoke, even when phonically identical. It is in this sense that obscenity becomes disturbational: its use erases a boundary between imitation and reality, and the art is disturbing because the reality it releases is itself disturbing. The famous first line of Alfred Jarry's *Ubu Roi* exploded into reality when voiced by the actor who stood before the audience and said, "Merdre!" Of course, "Merdre" is not the word it sounds like— "Merde"—but it sounds like it is, and the word it sounded like was not allowed in the stage vocabulary of the period: it could not be used representationally because it had, as it were, to be real, and "Merdre" in fact was like the lighted match at the gasworks, causing a kind of riot and melting the relationship between play and audience—which is what disturbational art aspires in principle to do.

For me the paradigm of this art, something it is difficult to imagine being banalized away, is the famous and frightening work *Deadman*, by Chris Burden, of 1972. Burden had himself enclosed in a sack and placed onto a freeway in California: a deadly pun by "corpse" on *corpus*. Burden could have been killed, knew he could have been killed, meant this fact to be part of the work and responded to in responding to the work. It did not happen, but it could have—without violating the boundaries of the work because the work incorporated those boundaries as part of its substance. It would be like exhibiting a work called "Bomb" at some future Biennial, consisting of a bomb, and where audience, curators, and artist all know it could go off at any time. This would be an exact illustration of Vito Acconci's generalized artistic intention of "setting up a field in which the audience was, so they became part of what I was doing." Knowing it was there, one would have to make an existential decision to visit the exhibition. It would not be like: "Shall we go to the Whitney or for a walk or stay home and read?" but more like "Shall we play Russian roulette, or make love without contraception, or drive full speed at one another to see who swerves first?" And ordinarily our involvement with art is not of this order: we are therefore in a very different artistic space than anything the philosophy of art has equipped us to construe as one of the possibilities of art, internal to something being a work of art.

Ubu Roi looks retrospectively innocent, and so, for different reasons, does the whittling away of himself of poor Rudolph Schwartzkogler, who died in 1969 of self-administered mutilations. Schwartzkogler seems somehow not to have known where to draw the line he meant to overstep in the name of disturbation, and to have been a kind of fool. And perhaps because of the certainty of the consequences, rather than simply the risk, as in Chris Burden's case. A well-known sculptor once made a work composed of heavy steel plates precariously balanced and held in place by friction. One was supposed to enter it to experience the space it created, but at the risk of having it collapse, and indeed someone was killed. This was in a museum where school-children are taken to experience art: it was like a loaded pistol, but though lethal, it was disturbational only if taking the chance of being flattened was meant as part of the experi-ence. Otherwise it was a possible consequence of a work indifferent to what happened to its audience, which is not out of character for the artist in question, and not disturba-tional at all.

These are extreme cases. They disturbate in the direction of life, though there are works which disturbate in the direc-tion of art, which was possible when art was believed sacred and fine and beautiful. Rimbaud's words "One evening I sat Beauty on my knees and found her bitter. And I injured her" expresses a hostility that often surfaced against Beauty and works defined by their beauty. It was in this spirit that Du-champ drew moustaches on the Mona Lisa—or on her im-ages. Or perhaps that Rauschenberg erased the drawing of De Kooning, which had to be a *good* drawing if it was to have the intended effect. The aura of danger, of risk, in any case ac-companies this strange domain of artistic expression, and part of experiencing is not knowing what will happen to us, since the contract that defines our rights as an audience is cancelled. And for exactly this reason the artist also does not know what is going to happen to her: instability makes vol-atile boundaries that nondisturbational art takes for granted. Will she be pelted, struck, stripped? This can happen without violating the conventions because this art exists in order that these conventions be suspended. But of course it is parasitic on these conventions, which infuses it with a paradox, and distinguishes it from art which happens merely to disturb, like Golub's, or which has real effects not part of itself, like the riots induced by the plays of J. M. Synge at the Abbey Theater in Dublin, or, to take a more complex case, the use by an artist of an incendiary content, or a content perceived as incendiary, and which may provoke a disturbance on ac-count of that. I am thinking of the patriotic operas of Verdi, but I am disinclined to rank *Simon Boccanegra,* or for the matter *The Playboy of the Western World,* as disturbational art, and it is perhaps worth trying to find out why. Perhaps it is because, in the case of the Abbey Theater audiences, it was they who traduced the boundaries without their doing so being part of the work nor in consequence a collaboration with the author. In the case of Verdi, who could scarcely have been unaware of the impact his operas were to have, he nonetheless insisted that it was merely art, which enabled him to make a political statement while standing immune from the effects it was almost certain to cause. His gesture and attitude bear comparison with that of guerrillas who defy their enemies to bomb the hospital they in fact are using to store weapons: they are not morally culpable if the enemy commits the atrocity of bombing a clearly marked hospital! No: in disturbational art, the artist is not taking refuge behind the conventions: he is opening a space which the conventions are designed to keep closed.

Let me revert to the moment, cataclysmic for the history of culture, when the Renaissance paradigm began to crumble. There was a wide spectrum of artistic response. On the one wing, as I seek to demonstrate in "The End of Art," art sought to merge with its own philosophy, seeing its task to be primarily that of providing an account of its essence which it began to think was defined by providing just such an account. Conceptual art was a deflected effort at realizing this program. Central in the spectrum were the various efforts at what we must think of as essentialisms, the alchemistic quest for pure art, for what would be left once we stripped away all those factors which were part of the discredited Renaissance paradigm itself. Here we find generic abstraction, which is a crude way of dealing with the Renaissance paradigm by mere subtraction, as it were, erasing that which made its overthrow possible, namely images of perceptual reality. Other responses in much the same spirit if less conceptually crude would have been: that the painting (the product) is painting (the process), which is largely the philosophy that came to vindicate the painting of the New York School, given the misnomer of Abstract Expressionism; that paintings are their own surfaces, so that any departure from flatness is a betrayal of the essence of this art; that the painting is the material substance of its execution, namely pigment, canvas, support; and of course the various minimalisms, since minimality is the metaphor for the search for the essence of art which has to be minimal since anything extrinsic to that essence is a violation. As against these efforts were those that refused to acknowledge the collapse of the paradigm and which therefore opposed the efforts that presupposed this by becoming illusionistic in a mad-dog kind of way, Op Art being a short-lived, literal version of this, but the various new realisms being likelier exemplars. Commercialisms of course operated from without, especially after the 1960s, when the art market began to be a central actor in the artworld, but I am seeking here a kind of philosophical overview, and crediting artists with searching, almost in the spirit of laboratory scientists, for an essence which would immunize art against the catastrophe in self-identity which the death of the paradigm revealed as a vivid possibility: that catastrophe was perceived as due to our not knowing what art really is, and believing it to be identical with what in fact is one of its incidental forms. In a way, modern art collaborated in bringing about the end of art in my sense of the term.

Now the art of disturbation belongs somewhere along this spectrum, and part of its paradox lies in the fact that it shares in its impulses the conceptual sophistications that mark modern art as a movement, but it aims at something much more primitive: it aims at reconnecting art with those dark impulses out of which art might be believed to have orginated and which art came more and more to stifle: it is a regressive posture, undertaking to recover a stage of art where art itself was almost like magic—like deep magic, making dark possibilities real, rather than shallow or illusory magic, where nothing really happens but it looks as though it has, where there is a repertoire of tricks rather than the invocation of alien forces from a space other than the one we occupy—summoning spirits from the vasty deep. The reversion to this beginning, to another and forgotten frame of mind, bears comparison with a parallel program in philosophy, that of the late Heidegger, who saw all philosophy after Socrates as a vast deviation from some direct encounter with Being, which Heidegger then took to reenact in writing of a different order altogether than the analytical forms which characterize western philosophical inscription since ancient times. Those strange late incantatory works seek to put the reader in direct contact with forgotten realities.

By magic, I have in mind that view of images, of course rarely held any longer, according to which the subject represented actually entered into its representations, so that theorists of the image, such as the iconodules of Byzantium, could speak of the mystical presence of the saint in the icon. You after all have to ask yourself why there has been at various times in history such intense controversy over the making of graven images, why there have been movements of iconoclasm at all. It is a struggle against the use of dark powers on the part of artists who, by making an image of x actually capture x in just the way men thought of capturing minotaurs or unicorns (anyone who believes zoos are educationally motivated has an underdeveloped sense of magic). Something of this magical theory, I am certain, enters into the intent of the death portrait, and into the explanation of the fact that mourners characteristically and unreflectingly seek to establish an image of the departed, as though death were magically overcome if the persona could be preserved. And how otherwise explain the worship of images—which would not be idolatry at all if the saint were literally *in* the picture—of the powers ascribed to various statues of the Virgin, of the *sacri bambini* to be found throughout Christendom, transradiated by the sort of holy presence that relics are supposed to house: as though one's form *were* a relic in this sense? Though I spoke of Duchamp putting moustaches on the Mona Lisa, of course it was a *postcard* that he modified, not the actual painting: but the image is present in the post-card, which is why Duchamp's gesture may be regarded as modestly disturbational, almost an act of vandalism.

As against the power of capturing realities, the mere ability to represent them, to hit off likeness, is not terribly interesting, and consists of tricks like those mastered by magicians whose aim is to entertain by fooling the eye. Once we perceive statues as merely designating what they resemble, where resemblance explains their form, rather than containing the reality through containing the form, a certain power is lost to art, granting that we have tended to define art by this loss—but this sort of definition may just be one of the forms of philosophical disenfranchisement the history of art reveals. In any case, disturbational art is an effort to reconnect with this magical frame of thought, long abandoned as a prerogative of image-makers, though, we saw, something like it is found in the elegant experiments of Johns. And my sense is that the power, or the belief that artists possessed it, was one of the things philosophers may have been afraid of when they turned to the ephemeralization of art as a matter of theory.

I want now to propose that this early, magical theory of images, easily confirmed in the history of Byzantine or Dutch iconoclasm, itself confirms a theory of dramatic representation which is given in a famous and beautiful speculation of Nietzsche's. Nietzsche proposes that classical tragedy is an evolution out of the dionysiac ritual, and consists in the insertion of a certain distance between audience—itself an evolution out of celebrants—and vision. In the ritual, the climactic moment was that in which the god himself made himself present, and it is this moment that the play is a civilized substitute for. The means by which the god was summoned were orgiastic: the dionysiac ritual was a dark celebration, an interval of frenzy in which everything civilized persons find repugnant was made possible and excused: it was frightening and, if you wish, disturbational, and undertaken for the sake of the epiphany. At that moment, the celebrants would be magically bonded with the god in their midst: all distinctions would fall away in an ecstasy of union. Greek tragedy reenacted this, but at the level of art rather than religious practice, and in effect this consisted in separating image from reality in a way modern theories of the image take for granted. The god is represented by an actor, the actor is not possessed by the god who makes himself present in the flesh and blood of the actor. We no longer think of the action on stage as more than distantly representing a distant presence. Even so, something of the expectation of magic must have remained in the theatrical experience of ancient times if we are to have any explanation of Aristotle's strange doctrine of catharsis, where something very profound happens to an audience, mystically purged as the original dionysiasts must have been by the climax of the enactment. It is reasonable to suppose people came to the theater for something like this to happen, rather than to enjoy a spectacle and have a good time. And who knows what associations with deep magic may not be woven into the patterns and attitudes of theater-going even today?

Since I am being ruthlessly speculative, let me draw at this point a contrast between theatrical audiences and movie audiences. The theater, if Nietzsche is right, is a complex transform out of some sacred precinct, in which the master of the ritual is transformed into tragic actor, the celebrants into an audience, and where instead of a god literally appearing to the latter by possessing the former, in a sense of "appearance" which does not contrast with reality, there are appearances of gods which *precisely* contrast with reality. We have both senses of "appearance" in English today: no one would say, when told that the president appeared at the inaugural ball, that he must not have been there, since it was only an appearance. But we do say that someone only appeared to love a person but did not really love him. There is illusion in the one case but not in the other. But the *movie house* is an evolution out of an optical device, the *camera obscura*, a box in which the appearances of the surrounding world were, as it were, stripped off the world and projected on the wall of the box through an aperture in the facing wall. The principles of the *camera obscura* were known to Aristotle, but by mid-nineteenth century there were boxes large enough to accommodate spectators among the distractions and amusements to be found by visitors to pleasure parks and seaside tivolis throughout Europe. Entering the boxes, they found images sundered from their correspondent realities—rollers and breakers and soddenly garmented figures in bathing machines—and this carries connotations of some magic thing having happened, as you may get a glimpse of in the Narrator's reflections on the magic lantern at the opening of *Swann's Way*. The images of course were evanescent, until Fox Talbot discovered how to capture them through the chemical mediation of silver iodide and sodium thiosulphate. The *camera obscura* has a fascinating double history, expanding into the box theater of the movie house and contracting into the box camera tourists in straw boaters aimed at one another against the scenic backdrops of the world. It is as though there were an internal linkage between the medium of cinematography and the locus of its exhibition. I abbreviate severely, skipping entirely the discoveries that made pictures *move*, but my concern is only to stress that movie houses have a very different origin and subsequent history than theaters do.

And this difference in origin is reflected in the difference between theatergoers and moviegoers, underwritten, I believe, by all manner of institutional evidence: we dress up to go to the theater, as to church, nor is there the ceremonial and celebratory spirit connected with moviegoing that seems natural to the theater: we drop into movie houses casually, at any point, and attending movies, save among solemn symposiasts from the *Cahiers de cinema*, is regarded as entertainment and distraction, even though there are profound films and simpy plays and sillier operas. The movie audience is *not* a transform out of a congregation. Its ancestor is the holiday throng, seeking respite from the press of daily reality rather than in pursuit of a higher reality and a revelation. One even may eat while watching movies, but this is frowned upon in the theater. The point is that one must resist a temptation to treat movies and plays as belonging to the same genre in virtue of each being seen in theaters and before audiences. It is as though the viewer of a film remains an individual, even if he sees the film with others, while the viewer of a play is a member of an audience, even if he should sit alone. The video cassette but emphasizes the difference, and though home viewers say that they sometimes want the experience of the movie house, this is almost certainly a matter of size and connected with certain felicities of projection not yet available at home. Or they mean they want to get away from the house, not that they want especially to enter another sort of space.

Now it seems to me that disturbatory art belongs to that kind of audience out of which the theatrical audience evolved, and means to regress to a more primitive relationship between actor and celebrants. The disturbatory artist aims to transform her audience into something pretheatrical, a body which relates to her in some more magical and transformational relationship than the defining conventions of the theater allow. And she means to achieve this by some transformation of herself, which consists in taking off the protective and powerfully dislocative atmosphere of theatrical distance and making contact with a reality. In some way the disturbatory artist sacrifices herself so that through her an audience may be transformed, perhaps only for a moment, as she becomes possessed by something alien. Hers, in brief, is an enterprise of restoring to art some of the magic purified out when art became *art*.

Of course the whole thing may simply explode into giggles. With our rational minds we find the theory that alone might legitimate these strange ambitions utterly discredited. But there is a subrational constituent in each of our psyches which art in ancient times managed to reach, and it is the reactivation of this contact—we see these impulses in Surrealism and Dada—at which disturbatory art aims. And this explains what is disturbing in disturbation, and why we need a word to nail it down. It is not ordinary disturbance with which we are dealing, and the shocking and outrageous are merely means to an end. It is the kind of disturbance that comes from the dim subperception that a dimension of our being is being signaled at a level below even the deepest levels of civilization. Greek civilization, if Nietzsche was right, owed itself to putting this all at a distance. We don't know what we are capable of, what we might do in response to the beckoning of the disturbatory artist: it is that sense of danger she insinuates which one might have felt as one crossed the terrifying boundaries of the precincts of Dionysus.

A few seasons ago there was a well-intentioned and in many ways successful attempt to reconstitute Malevich's *Victory over the Sun* at the Brooklyn Academy of Music. Faithful as the reconstitution was, it lacked and had to lack, just because it was faithful, that possibility of immediate contact with an audience at which Malevich aimed. It was in the end like looking through a glass aperture at electronically moving dinosaurs lovingly reconstituted for the edification of spectators who wonder what it looked like when dinosaurs shook the earth. Because of its being staged as a relic, for audiences who came to see it out of an antiquarian curiosity and a sense of aesthetic duty, who looked forward afterward to cheesecake at Juniors or drinks somewhere, it could not have worked. In some way the circumstances of its reenactment stand to the circumstances of its original innocence and hopefulness in something like the relationship Nietzsche describes between the classical theater and the original frenzy it meant to paralyze by the distance of artistic detachment. It is that distance disturbatory art wishes to remove.

I do not enjoy disturbatory art, perhaps because I am

always outside it and see it as pathetic and futile. And yet I am aware that there is an undeniable power in the concept of the artist as a kind of priest in a primitive ritual and of art itself as a miraculous intervention. And it is difficult to be dismissive of the courage of an artist who takes this frightening mission on. Nietzsche must have sensed this courage in Wagner, and hoped that Bayreuth would recreate the pre-theatrical sublimities of Greece, and touch elements in the psyche stifled by reason. Recreation, as we know, proved to be—recreation. Bayreuth was a profoundly disillusioning experience for Nietzsche, as it would have been for anyone who held these improbable ideals. If Richard Wagner could not bring it off, neither, I dare say, can Laurie Anderson, but the possibility remains too tantalizing finally to vanish from our ambition. Disturbatory art nevertheless goes against the historical grain, if my hegelian construction of the history of art is correct, but it reminds us of what this highly and increasingly philosophized enterprise had to grow out of.

VII.

Philosophy as/and/of Literature

By displaying what is subjective, the work, in its whole
presentation, reveals its purpose as existing *for* the subject,
for the spectator, and not on its own account. The spectator
is, as it were, in it from the beginning, is counted in with
it, and the work exists only for this point, i.e., for the
individual apprehending it.

—G. W. F. Hegel, *Aesthetics*.

*Delivered as my presidental address to the Eastern Division of the
American Philosophical Association in Boston, on December 28, 1983,
this essay appeared first in* Grand Street *and then in the* Proceedings
of the American Philosophical Association. *It copes with the effort
to turn philosophy itself into a form of art, at least as a genre of
literature, a brilliant if abortive move which would have made the
philosophical disenfranchisement of art self-disenfranchising, which is
clearly the desired aim of Jacques Derrida, who surfaces toward the
end. The title is a parody of the latter's signature willfulness with
punctuation. The epigraph is from Hegel,* Werke, *15:28; translated as*
Aesthetics: Lectures on Fine Art, *T. M. Knox, tr. (Oxford: Oxford
University Press, 1975), p. 806.*

OUR DISCIPLINE SEEMS so singular a crossbreed of art and
science that it is somewhat surprising that only lately has it

seemed imperative to some that philosophy be viewed as literature: surprising and somewhat alarming. Of course so much has been enfranchised as literature in recent times that it would have been inevitable that literary theorists should have turned from the comic strip, the movie magazine, the disposable romance—from science fiction, pornography, and graffiti—to the texts of philosophy, this in virtue of a vastly widened conception of the text which enables us to apply the strategies of hermeneutical interpretation to bus tickets and baggage checks, want ads and weather reports, laundry lists and postage cancellations, savings certificates and address books, medical prescriptions, pastry recipes, olive oil cans and cognac labels—so why *not* meditations, examinations, and critiques? Admittedly this is not the exalted sense of literature we have in mind in speaking of philosophy as an art, but even if we retain the normative connotations of the term, there is something disturbing in the fact that this particular face of philosophy should have now become visible enough that we should have been enjoined to treat its texts as a particular literary genre. For, after all, the imperatives which have governed the transformation of philosophy into a profession have stressed our community with the sciences. Were a kind of semiotic egalitarianism to direct us to regard as so many texts the papers which regularly appear in the *Physical Review,* their literary dimension must seem deeply secondary, as ours has always seemed to us to be: so to treat it suddenly as primary has to be unsettling.

Philosophy-as-literature carries implications in excess of the claim that philosophical texts have at times a degree of literary merit. We take a remote satisfaction that some of us—Strawson, Ryle, or Quine, let alone Santayana, Russell, and James—write distinguished prose, and we would all regard as astute a teacher of English who took pages from any of these as compositional paradigms. Still, our tendency is to regard style, save to the degree that it enhances perspicuity, as adventitious and superfluous to that for the sake of which we finally address these texts: as mere *Farbung,* to use Frege's dismissive term. So to rotate these texts in such a way that the secondary facets catch the light of intellectual concern puts what we regard as the primary facets in shadow: and to acquiesce in the concept of philosophy-as-literature just now seems tacitly to acquiesce in the view that the austere imperatives of philosophy-as-science have lost their energy. Considering what has been happening to texts when treated in recent times, our canon seems suddenly fragile, and it pains the heart to think of them enduring the frivolous sadism of the deconstructionist. But the perspective of philosophy-as-literature is an uncomfortable one for us to occupy, quite apart from these unedifying violations.

Consider the comparable perspective of the Bible-as-literature. Certainly it can be read as such, its poetry and narrative responded to as poetry and narrative, its images appreciated for their power and its moral representations as a kind of drama. But to treat it so is to put at an important distance the Bible considered as a body of revelations, of saving truths and ethical certitudes: a text of which a thinker like Philo could believe that everything in it and nothing outside of it is true. So some fundamental relationship to the book will have changed when it sustains transfer to the curriculum as "living literature." Of course some aspect of its style has from the beginning of its historical importance played a role in biblical epistemology. The language of the Koran is said so to transcend in its beauty the powers of human expressiveness as virtually to guarantee its own claim to have been dictated by an angel and to be, not even metaphorically, the word of God: so its style is taken to be the best evidence for its truth. Biblical writing, by contrast, was taken to be the record of human witnesses, and much of it was so offensive to literary taste that it had to be true; a second century apologist writes: "When I was giving my most earnest attention to discover the truth I happened to meet with certain barbaric writings . . . and I was led to put faith in these by the unpretending cast of the language." Origen, admitting the stylistic inferiority of Scripture by specific comparison with Plato, finds in this evidence that it is exactly the word of God, since if written by men it would be classier: its rudeness is a further weapon for confounding the wise. "However roughly, as regards mere authorship, my book should be got up," Poe has his fictional hero write in the arch foreword to *The Narrative of Arthur Gordon Pym*, "its very uncouthness, if there were any, would give it all the better chance of being received as truth." That plain prose has a better chance of being received true is a stylistic maxim not unknown in adopting a philosophical diction—think of Moore—but my point is only that there is a profound contrast between taking the Bible as literature and viewing it as the Word, and I would suspect disjoint classes of passages to become prominent depending on which view we take. The remaining music of the Bible must count as small compensation when the truth-claims made on its behalf are no longer felt to be compelling, and something like this contrast arises with philosophy-as-literature set against philosophy-as-truth. On the other hand it provides an occasion to reflect, as I shall do briefly, on how philosophical truth has been regarded if we approach philosophy for the moment as though it were a genre of literature: it enables us to see how we construed truth when we hadn't thought of ourselves as producing literature. And so we may reflect on the ways in which the dimensions of our professional being are connected.

For a period roughly coeval with that in which philosophy attained professionalization, the canonical literary format has been the professional philosophy paper. Our practice as philosophers consists in reading and in writing such papers, in training our students to read and write them, in inviting others to come read us a paper, to which we respond by posing questions that in effect are editorial recommendations, typically incorporated and acknowledged in the first or last footnote of the paper, in which we are exempted from such errors and infelicities as may remain, and thanked for our helpful suggestions. The journals in which these papers finally are printed, whatever incidental features useful to the profession at large they may carry, are not otherwise terribly distinct from one another, any more than the papers themselves characteristically are: if, under the constraints of blind review, we black out name and institutional affiliation, there will be no internal evidence of authorial presence, but only a unit of pure philosophy, to the presentation of which the author will have sacrificed all identity. This implies a noble vision of ourselves as vehicles for the transmission of an utterly impersonal philosophical truth, and it implies a vision of philosophical reality as constituted of isolable, difficult, but not finally intractable problems, which if not altogether soluble in fifteen pages more or less, can be brought closer to resolution in that many pages. The paper is then an impersonal report of limited results for a severely restricted readership, consisting of those who have some use for that result, since they are engaged with the writers of the papers in a collaborative enterprise, building the edifice of philosophical knowledge. It is perfectly plain that the implied vision of philosophical reality, as well as of the form of life evolved to discover it and the form of literature in which it is suitable to represent it, are closely modeled on the view of reality, life, and literature which composes what Thomas Kuhn has instructed us to think of as normal science. Mastery of the literary form is the key to success in the form of life, bringing tenure and the kind of recognition which consists in being invited to read papers widely and perhaps the presidency of one or another division of the American Philosophical Association. These practical benefits aside, no one could conceivably be interested in participating in the form of life defined by the literary form in issue, were it not believed that this is the avenue of philosophical truth. It is less obviously a matter of agreement that philosophical truth is defined by this being believed to be the way to find it.

It is not my purpose here to criticize a form of life in

which I, after all, participate, nor to criticize the format of
speech and writing which, after all, reinforces the virtues of
clarity, brevity, and competence in those compelled to use it.
I only mean to emphasize that the concept of philosophical
truth and the form of philosophical expression are internally
enough related that we may want to recognize that when we
turn to other forms we may also be turning to other concep-
tions of philosophical truth.

Consider the way in which we address our predecessors,
for example. A lot of what I have read on Plato reads much as
though he to whom the whole of subsequent philosophy
since is said to be so many footnotes, were in effect a footnote to himself, and being coached to get a paper accepted by
The Philosophical Review. And a good bit of the writing on
Descartes is by way of chivying his argumentation into notations we are certain he would have adopted had he lived to
appreciate their advantages, since it is now so clear where he
went wrong. But in both cases it might at least have been
asked whether what either writer is up to can that easily be
separated from forms it may have seemed inevitable that the
work be presented in, so that the dialogue or meditation
flattened into conventional periodical prose might not in the
process have lost something central to those ways of writing.
The form in which the truth as they understood it must be
grasped just might require a form of reading, hence a kind of
relationship to those texts, altogether different from that appropriate to a paper, or to what we sometimes refer to as a
"contribution." And this because something is intended to
happen to the reader other than or in addition to being
informed. It is after all not simply that the texts may lose
something when flattened into papers: life may have lost
something when philosophy is flattened out to the production and transmission of papers, noble as the correlative vision is. So addressing philosophy as literature is not meant to
stultify the aspiration to philosophical truth so much as to
propose a caveat against a reduced concept of reading, just
because we realize that more is involved even in contempo-

rary, analytical philosophy than merely stating the truth: to get at that kind of truth involves some kind of transformation of the audience, and the acquiescence in a certain form of initiation and life.

I cannot think of a field of writing as fertile as philosophy has been in generating forms of literary expression, for ours has been—to use a partial list I once attempted—a history of dialogues, lecture notes, fragments, poems, examinations, essays, aphorisms, meditations, discourses, hymns, critiques, letters, summae, encyclopedias, testaments, commentaries, investigations, tractatuses, *Vorlesungen, Aufbauen,* prolegomena, parerga, *pensées,* sermons, supplements, confessions, sententiae, inquiries, diaries, outlines, sketches, commonplace books, and, to be self-referential, addresses, and innumerable forms which have no generic identity or which themselves constitute distinct genres: *Holzwege,* Grammatologies, Unscientific Postscripts, Genealogies, Natural Histories, Phenomenologies, and whatever the *World as Will and Idea* may be or the posthumous corpus of Husserl, or the later writings of Derrida, and forgetting the standard sorts of literary forms—e.g., novels, plays, and the like, which philosophers have turned to when gifted those ways. One has to ask what cognitive significance is conveyed by the fact that the classic texts of China are typically composed of conversational bits, a question brought home vividly to me when a scholar I respect complained that it is terribly hard to get any propositions out of Chuang Tzu: for this may be the beginning of an understanding of how that elusive sage is to be addressed, and what it means to read him. Responding to a review of *The Realm of Truth* by his amenuensis, Santayana wrote: "It is well that now you can take a holiday: which doesn't exclude the possibility of returning to them with freshness of judgement and apperception. Perhaps then you might not deprecate my purple passages, and might see, which is the historical fact, that they are not applied ornaments but natural growths and *realizations* of the thought moving previously in a limbo of verbal abstractions."

It is arguable that the professional philosophical paper is an evolutionary product, emerging by natural selection from a wild profusion of forms darwinized into oblivion through maladaptation, stages in the advance of philosophy toward consciousness of its true identity, a rockier road than most. But it is equally arguable that philosophers with really new thoughts have simply had to invent new forms to convey them with, and that it may be possible that from the perspective of the standard format no way into these other forms, hence no way into these systems or structures of thought, can be found. This claim may be supported, perhaps, by the consideration that pretty much the only way in which literature of the nonphilosophical kind has impinged upon philosophical awareness has been from the perspective of truth-or-falsity. The philosopher would cheerfully consign the entirety of fiction to the domain of falsehood but for the nagging concern that a difference is to be marked between sentences which miss the mark and sentences which have no mark to miss and are threatened in consequence of prevailing theories of meaning with meaninglessness. Some way must therefore be found for them to have meaning before they can be dismissed as false, and pretty much the entirety of the analytical—and I may as well add the phenomenological—corpus has been massively addressed to the question of fictive reference. Literature sets up obstacles to the passage of semantical theories which would go through a great deal more easily if literature did not exist. By assessing it against the concept of reference, literature derives what intellectual dignity philosophy can bestow, with the incidental benefit that if literature is merely a matter of relating words to the world, well, if philosophy is literature it is meaningful, providing it can only show how. And philosophy's way of relating literature to reality may make philosophy-as-literature one with philosophy-as-truth.

This is scarcely the place to tell the chilling tale of fictional reference, in part because it seems not to have reached an end, there being no accepted theory of how it works. But if there ever was an argument for philosophy as a kind of literature, it might be found in the extravagant ontological imagination of semantical theorists in proposing things for fictive terms to designate. Since *Don Quixote* is meaningful, "Don Quixote" must refer—not, to be sure, to some specific addled Spaniard in La Mancha, but to Don Quixote himself, a subsistent entity, which *Don Quixote* can now be about in just the way it would if he were indeed an addled Spaniard in La Mancha. How such subsistent entities confer meaning, or at least how they explain the fact that we grasp it, was never particularly explained, causal transactions between the domain of subsistent entities and existent entities such as we being surely ruled out of question. This problem is aggravated when we purge the universe of fictive beings by waving a quinian wand which changes names into predicates, Don Quixote becoming the x that quixotizes all over the y that lamanchas. The prodigality complained of in manufacturing entities to order is evidently unnoticed when it comes to manufacturing predicates to order, and the change from *Gegenstände* to *Gedanke* leaves the question of meaning and its being grasped about as dark as ever—nor is the matter especially mitigated when we allow *Don Quixote* to pick a possible world to be about, for the relationship of it to ours and finally to us remains as obscure as that between Don Quixote and us when he was a homeless wraith, an ontological ghost wandering in worlds undreamt of by poets. From this point of view Professor Goodman's elegant theory of secondary extensions is particularly welcome, first from the perspective of ontology, since secondary extensions are comprised of things we can put our hands on, like inscriptions, and secondly from the point of view of epistemology, since pictures play a prominent part in the secondary extension of a term and we in fact begin our adventures into literature with picture books. It does on the other hand throw an immense semantical burden on illustrated editions and the like; and tangles us in puzzles of its own, since the set of pictures ostensibly *of* the same thing may look so little alike that we may have severe doubts as to what their subject would look like if it existed, while pictures of altogether different subjects may look so alike that we could not tell them apart were they to be real. Whether we must ascend to tertiary extensions and beyond, and how these would solve our further problems, are matters not to be taken up here, for the question I want to raise is why, whichever of these theories is true, we, as readers, should have the slightest interest in *Don Quixote* if what it is about is an unactualized thin man in a region of being I would have no reason to know about save for the interventions of semantical theory: or if it were about the x that quixotizes (there being none) or a set of possible worlds other than my own, or primarily about nothing but secondarily about such things as a set of engravings by Gustav Doré.

I raise the question because literature, certainly in its greatest exemplars, seems to have something important to do with our lives, important enough that the study of it should form an essential part of our educational program, and this is utterly unexplained if its meaning is a matter of its reference, and its candidate referenda are as bizarre a menagerie of imaginabilia as the fancy of man has framed. And it may be that when we show the kind of connection there is, there will not be a problem of the sort to which semantical theory has been so elaborate a response. Well, it may be said, this might simply remove literature from the sphere of philosophical concern, a welcome enough removal but for the fact that it might remove philosophy itself from the domain of philosophical concern if philosophy itself is literature. And my insinuation has been that the sorts of things philosophy has laid down to connect literature in order to give it meaning—*Gegenstände*, intensions, fictive worlds—are themselves as much in need of ontological redemption as the beings to whose rescue they were enlisted—Don Quixote, Mr. Pickwick, Gandolf the Grey. To believe we can save fiction by means of fiction is one of the endearing innocences of a discipline that takes pride in what it likes to think is its skeptical circumspection.

Semantical theory does the best it can in striving to connect literature to the world through what after all are the only kinds of connections it understands: reference, truth, instantiation, exemplification, satisfaction, and the like, and if this means distorting the universe in order that it can *receive* literary representations, well, this has never been reckoned a heavy price for philosophy to pay—has not been reckoned a price at all but a creative opportunity—and it remains to the credit of this enterprise that it at least believes that *some* connection between literature and the world is required. In this it contrasts with literary theory as currently practiced, which impugns philosophical preoccupations with sematical ligatures as but a further instance of what one leading theoretician dismisses as the Referential Fallacy. Literature does not refer at all to reality, according to this view, but at best to other literature, and a concept of *intertextuality* is advanced according to which a literary work is to be understood, so far as referentiality facilitates understanding, only in terms of other works a given work refers to, so that no one equipped with less than the literary culture of the writer of a work up for interpretation can be certain of having understood the work at all. There is certainly something to this view if Northrop Frye is correct in claiming, of Blake's line "O Earth, O Earth return" that "though it contains only five words and only three different words"—five tokens and three types, as we might more briskly say—"it contains also about seven direct allusions to the Bible." The author of the Referential Fallacy, whom I prefer for somewhat complex reasons to refer to simply as R—he after all speaks for his profession—assures us that "the poetic text is self-sufficient." But "if there is external reference, it is not to reality—far from it! Any such reference is to other texts." This extreme view merits some examination if only for its vivid opposition to the standard philosophical view.

Consider one of his examples, the last line of Wordsworth's poem "Written in March," which goes: "Small clouds are sailing, / Blue skies prevailing, / The rain is over and done." This line, together with the title, might lead the

reader to suppose that the poem refers to the end of winter
and expresses the poet's gratitude that Spring has come at
last—but this easy reading is, according to R, quite seriously
and fallaciously wrong: it refers in fact to the Song of Songs,
from which Wordsworth's line is taken verbatim, and is in
fact a fragment of the biblical line which begins "For lo! The
winter is past. . . " Now it hardly can be doubted that Wordsworth knew the Song of Songs, and it is certain that literary
scholarship, in explaining the sources of the poem, will refer
to it as an ultimate source for the last line. Perhaps every line
or every phrase in a poem may be explained with reference
to something in the literary culture of the writer. But not
every literary effect necessarily *refers* to its causes, and there
is a considerable difference between understanding a poem,
which may require understanding its references when it
makes them, and understanding the provenances of a poem,
which is quite another matter: it is specialist knowledge, and
likely incidental to understanding a poem.

Let me offer an illustration from another art, in part to
make my argument more general, in part to confirm a claim
about pictorial semantics. Raphael's beautiful *Madonna della
sedia* is composed within a circular frame—a *tondo*—not, as
Gombrich points out, because Raphael one day seized a
handy barrelhead in order to paint up an innkeeper's
daughter who charmed him, together with her pretty child,
as Madonna and Infant, which is the tour guide's lovely
explanation; but rather because, like many of his contemporaries, Raphael was excited by some recently exhibited drawings of Leonardo, among them some circular compositions.
Every painter in the region would have known about those
drawings, and hence the provenance of Raphael's painting,
but for all that Raphael was not referring to the drawings
which inspired him. By contrast, the American painter Benjamin West did a portrait of his wife and son in *tondo* form,
her garment the garment of Raphael's Madonna, not as a
copy of but *in reference to* Raphael's painting. It was an exceedingly pretentious reference, depicting his wife as

Madonna, his child as the Baby Jesus, *his* painting as the
Madonna della sedia, and himself as Raphael. But to understand the painting is to understand those allusions, for he is
representing his family *as* the Holy Pair *as* depicted by
Raphael, and a very self-exalting metaphor is being transacted. (What a humiliation to have had this hopeful vision
deaccessioned by the Reynolds' collection in exchange for a
merely typical Thomas Cole!)

It was a triumph of art-historical scholarship to demonstrate the unmistakable use made by Manet of an arrangement of figures in an engraving by Marcantonio Raimondi in
setting the figures in his *Déjeuner sur l'herbe.* This by no
means excludes the possibility, or rather the fact, that Manet
was representing friends of his, wits and demimondaines,
enjoying an elegant outing. Of course it is a different painting depending upon whether he was referring to or merely
using Raimondi's work. If he was referring to it, then his
subject is *that* outing *as* a feast of the gods, which is the
subject of the original engraving. Raimondi was the most
famous engraver of his age (as well as a notorious forger), but
in Manet's world he was doubtless too obscure for such an
allusion to be made, by contrast perhaps with biblical references in Wordsworth's world: and probably obviousness is a
condition of allusion as banality is a condition of validity in
the enthymene.

But even so Manet's use of that engraving must be distinguished from a use made by the American painter John
Trumbell, in his famous portrait of General Washington with
his horse, of a certain preexisting form of horse representation. Far from being the finely observed depiction of Washington's elegant steed, Washington's horse, as shown, is but
one in a long historical sequence of similar horses which Leo
Steinberg has traced back to a Roman cameo, and which
probably could be traced even further. Still, it is Washington
with his horse that is being referred to, and not any member
of this series, each of which but conforms to a pattern. The
pattern, which may be an example of what Gombrich speaks

of as a *schema*, is a very satisfactory way of representing horses, which are, as we know, very difficult to observe—until Muybridge nobody knew whether all four legs were altogether off the ground in gallop—and yields up a kind of representational *apriori* of a sort whose narrative and lyrical counterparts may be found in literature and, though this is not my topic, there may be profound similarities with scientific representations as well.

In all these cases and countless others, reference to the world works together with references to other art, when there are such references, to make a complex representation: so why should or must it be different in the case of Wordsworth? R writes thus: "The key word—*winter*—absent from Wordsworth, is the matrix penetrating every Spring detail in the poem . . . now perceived as the converse of an image that has been effaced, so that the poem is not a direct depiction of reality, but a negative version of a latent text on the opposite of Spring." This is the kind of hermeneutic contortion that earns interpreters of literature distinguished chairs in universities—the kind that argue, for example, that *Hamlet* is a negative version of a latent text about Fortinbras, the *true* hero of the play, perceived now as comedy rather than tragedy; since the hero is alive at the end, and making Shakespeare a clever forerunner of Tom Stoppard. But my concern is not to argue with the interpretation but with the "so" to which R is not entitled: a proper interpretation would have to show why Wordsworth referred to the season through the medium of a biblical allusion if in fact it was an allusion and not a cliché of the sort that has simply entered language the way so much of *Hamlet* has that a student is said to have criticized it for being too full of clichés, though a pretty exciting story. And what of the Song of Songs itself, if poetry: is *it* about winter, or, to use the other option offered us, altogether self-contained?

In a famous letter to his mistress, Louise Collet, Flaubert lays out his own ideal as an artist: "What I should like to write is a book about nothing, a book dependent upon nothing external, which would be held together by the internal strength of its style, just as the earth, suspended in the void, depends upon nothing external for its support: a book which would have almost no subject, or at least in which the subject would be invisible, if such a thing is possible." Flaubert's astronomy is appalling, and if R is right he could not have failed of his purpose, all literature, just so far as it is literature, being about nothing. Or at best about other literature, work holding work in referential orbit, to give Flaubert a happier physical metaphor, but basically untethered to reality. The question is, what considerations recommend the guaranteed irrelevancy of literature to life?

"In everyday language," the author of the Referential Fallacy writes, "words seem to refer vertically, each to the reality it seems to render, like the labels on a barellhead, each a semantic unit. While in literature the unit of meaning is the text itself. The reciprocal effects of its words on one another, as members of a finite network, replace the vertical semantical relationship with a lateral one, forged along the written line, tending to cancel the dictionary meanings of the words."

Now I want to applaud the concept of a text as a network of reciprocal effects. Not original with R, of course, it has entered our world from European sources, making an immense impact upon literary theorists while leaving philosophy so far untouched. I feel that were the concept of the text to become as central in analytical philosophy as the sentence has been since Frege gave it primacy, or as the term has been since Aristotle, a vast world for philosophical research will have opened up. For the concept of the text is considerably wider than literary texts alone. It applies to musical compositions and to architectural structures, artforms whose referentiality has been in occasional question, and to personalities, whole lives in the biographical sense of the term, families, villages, cultures, things for which the question of referentiality has hardly been raised at all. And the expression "a network of reciprocal effects" will come to be exchanged for a class of relationships as various and perhaps as important as those which bind sentences into arguments, and which have been so massively explored in contemporary philosophical thought. Even so, it is altogether compatible with being united through a network of reciprocal effects that a literary work should refer, as it were extratextually, though the reference may be complicated as much by intra- as by intertextual references. The "Prelude" and "Finale" of *Middlemarch* refer reciprocally, as well as to the novel they frame, and both refer or allude to Saint Theresa, herself not a text save in so wide a sense as to make R's theory timid and disappointing. They refer to her to provide a metaphor for Dorothea Brooks—Miss Brooks as erotic ascetic perhaps— proving that her character has remained constant through two marriages, and saying finally something deep about the narrow space there is, after all, for being different from what we are.

But this goes well beyond what philosophers have wanted to say in supposing *Middlemarch* refers, say, to a world of its own or to some fleshless subsistent woman, Dorothea Brooks. And it goes well beyond what R will allow, who leaves us with the same question philosophical discussions of fictional reference did—namely, why should we be interested in *Middlemarch*? Why, since not ourselves literary scholars, should we concern ourselves with these intricate networks of reciprocal effects? "Because they are there" was not even a good reason for climbing mountains, but I am struck by the fact that philosophers seem only to understand vertical and literary theorists, if R is right, only horizontal references. On this coordinate scheme it is difficult to locate literature in the plane of human concern at all. Clearly we need a *z* coordinate, must open a dimension of reference that neither vertical nor horizontal reference quite reveal, if we are to get an answer. In what remains of this essay, that is what I want to begin to do.

"The distinction between historian and poet is not in the

one writing prose and the other verse," Aristotle writes, helpfully as always. "You might put the work of Heroditus into verse and it would still be a species of history." Though he neglects the reverse possibility, I take Aristotle to mean that one ought to be *unable* to tell by mere examination of a text whether it is poetry or something else, which gives my own question an immediate philosophical structure. The form of a philosophical question is given—I would venture to say always, but lack an immediate proof—when indiscriminable pairs with nevertheless distinct ontological locations may be found or imagined found, and we then must make plain in what the difference consists or could consist. The classical case is matching dream experience with waking experience in such a way that, as Descartes required, nothing internal to either mode of experience will serve as differentiating criterion. So whatever internal criterion we in fact and, as it happens, preanalytically employ will be irrelevant to the solution of the problem—e.g., that dreams are vague and incoherent: for dreams may be imagined, and possibly had, which are as like waking experience as we require to void the criterion. So the difference must come in at right angles to the plane of what we experience, and philosophy here consists in saying what it can be. Kant discovers the same thing in moral theory, since he imagines it possible that a set of actions should perfectly conform to principle and yet have no moral worth, because that requires a different relationship to those principles than mere conformity, and outward observation cannot settle the matter. And Adeimanthus furnishes the stunning example which generates the *Republic,* of a perfectly just man whose behavior is indiscriminable from that of a man perfectly unjust: the example requires that justice be orthogonal to conduct, and entails as uniquely possible the kind of theory Plato gives us. Other examples lie ready to hand. The present state of the world is compatible with the world being any age at all, including five minutes old, and nothing on the surface of the world will arbitrate without begging the question. A mere bodily movement and a basic action might appear exactly alike, just as what we take to be an expression of a feeling may be but a kind of rictus. Nothing open to observation discriminates a pair of connected events, to use Hume's distinction, from a pair merely conjoined. And in my own investigations into the philosophy of art, I have benefited immensely from Duchamp's discovery that nothing the eye can reveal will arbitrate the difference between a work of art and a mere real thing which resembles it in every outward particular. So any proposed distinction based upon perceptual differences, even in the visual arts, will have proved, as with the linnaean system in botany, to be artificial, however useful in practice. Duchamp consigned all past theories to oblivion by proving that the problem was philosophical. And here is Aristotle, telling us that the difference between poetry and history does not lie on the surfaces of texts, and that distinguishing them is not an ordinary matter of classification but a philosophical matter of explanation.

It is indeed not at all difficult to imagine two quite sustained pieces of writing which belong to relevantly distinct genres, without there being so much difference as a semicolon. I once imagined a pair of indiscriminable texts, one a novel, one a piece of history. My colleague Stern, suppose, comes across an archive containing the papers of a Polish noblewoman of the last century, who died, characteristically, in a convent. Incredibly, she was the mistress of Talleyrand, of Metternich, of the young Garibaldi, of Jeremy Bentham, Eugene Delacroix, of Frederic Chopin, Czar Nicholas of Russia, and thought the great loves of her life were George Sand and the nubile Sarah Bernhardt. Published by Viking, the work wins the Pulitzer Prize in history in the same year as a novel with exactly the same name wins the prize in literature—*Maria Mazurka, Mistress of Genius*—written by Erica Jong, who was inspired to invent a heroine who dies, appropriately, in a convent, but who in her time had been the mistress of Talleyrand, Metternich, the younger Garibaldi, of Jeremy Bentham, Eugene Delacroix, of Frederic Chopin, Czar Nicholas of Russia, and thought the great loves of her life were George Sand and the nubile Sarah Bernhardt. Jong's novel, unfortunately, is too improbable, has too many characters, sprawls all over the place, as Jong is wont to do these days—and it bears critical comparison with Stern's marvelous book which manages to keep track of all its characters, is tightly regimented given the diversity of materials, and contains not a fact in excess. So Jong's book, to the despair of the author and Random House, is soon remaindered, and for $2.98 you can get a lot of pages which cannot be told apart from Stern's book, on special at $19.99 through the History Book Club—though none of Stern's readers would be caught dead reading a mere novel. Stern's book, of course, refers vertically, while Jong's, being a novel, is a network of reciprocal effects, and self-sustained or nearly so, characterized only by horizontal reference. I realize I am slipping out of philosophy into literature: but the point is that whatever is to mark the difference must survive examples such as these.

Aristotle's famous suggestion, of course, is that "poetry is something more philosophical and of graver import than history, since its statements are of the nature of universals, whereas those of history are singular." It is plain that this difference is not registered grammatically or syntactically, if the example just constructed is possible and in the aristotelian spirit. So there must be a way in which Jong's book, for all its failings, is universal, and in which Stern's book, splendid as it is as historiography, remains for just that reason singular—about that specific woman in just those steamy liaisons. On the other hand, there must be some way in which Jong's book, if universal and hence more philosophical than Stern's, is not quite so philosophical as philosophy itself is—otherwise the problem of construing philosophy as a form of literature would be solved at the cost of so widening philosophy, since nothing could be more philosophical than it, as to compass whatever Aristotle would consider poetry. In whatever way philosophy is to be literature, if it is to be literature at all, it must respect whatever differences

there may be with literature which is not philosophy, however necessarily philosophical it has to be in order to be
distinguished from mere history.

My own view is that philosophy wants to be more than
universal: it wants necessity as well: truth for all the worlds
that are possible. In this respect it contrasts with history, or
for that matter with science, concerned with the truths of just
this particular, uniquely actual world, and happy if it can
achieve that much. My contention here has been that philosophical semantics renders literature true of possible worlds,
to lapse into vernacular, in such a way that it would be history for any of them if actual instead of ours—as *Gulliver's
Travels* would just be anthropology for a world in which there
were Lilliputians instead of Melanesians. This, I am afraid, is
very close to Aristotle's own view, history dealing, according
to him, with the thing that has been, while poetry deals with
"a kind of thing that might be." And that sounds too much
like being true of a possible world to be comfortable with as
an analysis. I nevertheless believe there is a kind of universality to literature worth considering, different from this, and
I shall now try to say what it is in my own way, recognizing
that if philosophy is also literature, it might have to be universal and possibly even necessary in two kinds of ways.

The thought I want to advance is that literature is not
universal in the sense of being about every possible world
insofar as possible, as philosophy in its nonliterary dimension aspires to be, nor about what may happen to be the case
in just this particular world, as history, taken in this respect
as exemplificatory science, aspires to be, but rather about
each reader who experiences it. It is not, of course, about its
readers as a book about reading is, which happens incidentally to be about its readers just as a subclass of its subject,
but rather in the way in which, though you will look for him
in vain, Benjamin West's pretentious family portrait is about
him. He does not show himself in the manner of Velásquez in

Las Meninas, but still, the painting is about Benjamin West *as* Raphael *as* painter of the Holy Family, through an allusive and metaphoric identification: he informs the work as a kind of *dieu caché*. Well, I want to say that a literary work is about its readers in this metaphoric and allusive way, in an exact mirror image of the way West's painting is about him: in Hegel's wonderful thought, the work exists for the spectator and not on its own account: it exists, as he says, only for the individual apprehending it, so that the apprehension completes the work and gives it final substance. The difficult claim I am making can be put somewhat formally as follows: the usual analysis of universality is that $(x)Fx$ is via the mechanisms of natural deduction equivalent to a conjunction of all the values on x, true in the event each is F. The universality of literary reference is only that it is about each individual that reads the text at the moment that individual reads it, and it contains an implied indexical: each work is about the "I" that reads the text, identifying himself not with the implied reader for whom the implied narrator writes, but with the actual subject of the text in such a way that each work becomes a metaphor for each reader: perhaps the same metaphor for each.

A metaphor, of course, in part because it is literally false that I am Achilles, or Leopold Bloom, or Anna or Oedipus or King Lear or Hyacinth Robinson or Strether or Lady Glencora: or a man hounded by an abstract bureaucracy because of an unspecified or suspected accusation, or the sexual slave O, or the raft-rider responsible to a moral being an unspeakable nation refuses to countenance as a man, or the obsessive narrator of the violence of my ancestors which is my own violence since their story is in the end my story, or one who stands to Jay Gatsby as Jay Gatz stood to the same dream as mine of "love, accomplishment, beauty, elegance, wealth" (which is a list I just found in a marvelous story by Gail Godwin). It is literature when, for each reader I, I is the subject of the story. The work finds it subject only when read.

Because of this immediacy of identification, it is natural to think, as theorists from Hamlet upward have done, of literature as a kind of mirror, not simply in the sense of rendering up an external reality, but as giving me to myself for each self peering into it, showing each of us something inaccessible without mirrors, namely that each has an external aspect and what that external aspect is. Each work of literature shows in this sense an aspect we would not know was ours without benefit of that mirror: each discovers—in the eighteenth-century meaning of the term—an unguessed dimension of the self. It is a mirror less in passively returning an image than in transforming the self-consciousness of the reader who in virtue of identifying with the image recognizes what he is. Literature is in this sense transfigurative, and in a way which cuts across the distinction between fiction and truth. There are metaphors for every life in Herodotus and Gibbon.

The great paradigm for such transfiguration must be Don Quixote, Cervantes having to be credited not only with the invention of the novel but with discovering the perversion of its philosophy. Quixote is transformed, through reading romances, into an errant knight while his world is transformed into one of knightly opportunities, wenches turning into virgins and innkeepers into kings, nags into steeds and windmills into monsters. Yet it is a perversion of the relationship between reader and romance because Quixote's own sense of his identity was so antecedently weak that he failed to retain it through the transformation, and his own sense of reality was so weak that he lost his grip on the difference between literature and life. Or he read poetry as though it were history, so not philosophical but particular. He would be like those who, through reading Descartes, seriously come to believe that "they are kings while they are paupers, that they are clothed in gold and purple while they are naked; or imagine that their head is made of clay or that they are gourds, or that their bodies are glass." Or that there is an Evil Genius, or that there is no world or that the belief in material objects is misguided. These are failures to distinguish philosophy from life, whose counterpart in Cervantes induces an illusion so powerful that the distinction is lost: which may be a formula for happiness—living in an illusion—making *Don Quixote* genuinely comic.

I have encountered the tragic obverse of this, where one's sense of self is strong but one's sense of reality has become desperate through literature having thrown a bitter discrepancy into the relationship between the two. I knew a lady who discovered the truth from Proust's novel that she really was the Duchess of Guermantes, as unavailing, in her case, unfortunately, as the Prince's knowledge of who he really is, when a spell has nevertheless required that he live in the investitures of a frog. *Her* land was Combray and the Faubourg St. Germain, an air of wit and exquisite behavior and perfect taste—not the Upper West Side, falling plaster, children with colds, a distracted husband, never enough money and nobody who understood. Her moments of happiness came when reality on occasion agreed to cooperate with metaphor, when she could coincide with an alien grace, too ephemeral alas, leaving her with the dishes to clear and the bills to pay and a terrible exhaustion. Unlike Quixote, her illusions never were strong enough to swamp reality, only in a sense to poison it; and while she maintained that her greatest happiness consisted in reading Proust, in truth he only caused her anguish.

I should like to place the theorist R alongside these two readers of fiction, one of whom happens to be in fiction as well, since R himself could be a fictional being and "The Referential Fallacy" a fiction within a fiction, both of them created by me. In fact both the theorist and article are real. R is a man of great pride and passion, who has lived through times of extremity and has known, as much as anyone I know has known, the defining tribulations of the full human life. Surely he cannot have been drawn to literature simply to be a reader of literature through literature to literature, unless, like the professor in Mann's *Disorder and Early Sorrow*, he meant to draw a circle in order to exclude life. If it were a piece of literature, "The Referential Fallacy" would offer a metaphor of extreme dislocation, putting life as a whole beyond the range of reference, displaying an existence lived out in an infinite windowless library, where book sends us to book in a network of reciprocal relationships the reader can inhabit like a spider. Imagine that it had been written by Borges, whose life is almost like that, and included in *Ficciones*! But it in fact is by R and it gives us a misanalysis rather than a metaphor; it refers vertically to readers whose relationship to texts it gets wrong, rather than to the reader of the text whose life it metaphorically depicts. If this address were art, it would be a mirror only for R, who seeing his own image reflected back, might find his consciousness entrapped and mend his thought.

R's text, which I have sought to view once as literature and once as science, illustrates, since it is about reading, the two ways in which a text might refer to readers, and with these two modes of reference in mind, we may return to the *philosophy* as literature, not by way of treating philosophical texts as literature, which would be merely a conceit if they were not that, as R's text is not that, but by way rather of displaying one of the ways in which philosophy really does relate to life. *One* of the ways. There is a celebrated deconstructionist text which holds that philosophy must be treated as a genre of literature because it is ineluctably metaphoric, when in fact it only becomes interestingly metaphoric when it is first decided to treat it as literature, and that text begs just the question it has been taken by its enthusiasts to have settled. Metaphors have in common with texts as such that they do not necessarily wear their metaphoricity on their surfaces, and what looks like an image may really be a structural hypothesis as to how a reality we heretofore lack words for is to be understood. One mark of metaphors is their ineliminability, a feature which makes them paraintensional if not fully intensional. But in philosophical as in scientific writing, what looks like a metaphor in the beginning ends as a fact, and it may be eliminated in favor of a technical term, as Locke begins with the natural light—with "the candle within us"—and ends with the technical term *intuition*. So what appear to be metaphors, what have been taken by deconstructionists to be metaphors, belong to philosophy as science, rather than to philosophy as literature.

There is a view abroad, credited to Nietzsche, that in metaphor we have the growing edge of language, assimilating by its means the unknown to the known, where the latter must originally have been metaphor now grown cold and dessicated and taken for fact. It is difficult to understand how, on its own view, this process got started, but I think it must be appreciated as a transvaluational and necessarily paradoxical view, like saying that the first shall be last or that the meek shall inherit the earth, giving poetry the place science has presumed was its own. But it is a view lent credibility by the fact that structural hypotheses look enough like metaphors to be taken for metaphors by theorists resolved to view an activity like philosophy as largely if not altogether metaphorical. It is my own thought that philosophical texts are kept alive as metaphors when they have long since stopped seeming plausible as structural hypotheses, a tribute to their vivacity and power, their status as literature being a consolation prize for failing to be true. But this is to overlook the way in which philosophy just functions as literature does, not in the sense of extravagant verbal artifacts, but as engaging with readers in search of that sort of universality I have supposed to characterize literary reference: as being about the reader at the moment of reading through the process of reading. We read them as literature in this sense because, in Hegel's stunning thought, they exist for the reader who is "in them from the beginning." The texts require the act of reading in order to be complete, and it is as readers of a certain type that philosophical texts address us all. The wild variety of philosophical texts implies a correspondingly wild variety of possible kinds of readers, and hence of theories of what we are in the dimension of the reading. And each such text finds a kind of ontological proof of its claims through the fact that it can be read in the way it requires.

The most conspicuous example of such a text is obliged to be the *Meditations,* where the reader is forced to comeditate with the writer, and to discover in the act of comeditation his philosophical identity: he must be the kind of individual the text requires if he can read it, and the text must be true if it can be read. He finds himself there since he was in it from the beginning. How astonishing I find it that precisely those who insist that philosophy is merely a genre of literature offer readings of Descartes so external that the possibility of their being universal in the way literature demands is excluded from the outset. To treat philosophical texts after the manner of Derrida, simply as networks of reciprocal relationships, is precisely to put them at a distance from its readers so intraversable as to make it impossible that they be about us in the way literature requires, if my conjecture is correct. They become simply artifacts made of words, with no references save internal ones or incidental external ones. And reading them becomes external, as though they had nothing to do with us, were merely there, intricately wrought composites of logical lacework, puzzling and pretty and pointless. The history of philosophy is then like a museum of costumes we forget were meant to be worn.

The variety of philosophical texts, then, subtend a variety of philosophical anthropologies, and though each text is about the reader of it and so is a piece of literature by that criterion, it does not offer a metaphor but a truth internally related to the reading of it. Even now when textual innovativeness has abated in philosophy and all texts are pretty much alike, so much so that the address to the reader has thinned almost to nothingness, the reader in the act of reading exercises some control over what the text says, since what the text says must be compatible with its being read. A text, thus, which set out to prove the impossibility of reading would have a paradox of sorts on its hands. Less flagrantly, there are texts in philosophy, current reading among us, which if true would entail their own logical illegibility. And it is inconceivable that philosophers would have fallen into such incoherences if they had not, as it were, forgotten that their texts, in addition to being representations of a kind of reality, were things to be *read*. We pay a price for forgetting this in the current style of writing, since it enables us to depict worlds in which readers cannot fit. The propensity to overlook the reader goes hand in hand with the propensity to leave beings of the sort readers exemplify outside the world the text describes. Contemporary philosophies of mind, language, humanity may be striking examples of an oversight which is encouraged by a view of philosophical writing which makes the reader ontologically weightless: like some disembodied professional conscience. Science, often and perhaps typically, can get away with this, largely because, even when about its readers, it is not about them as readers, and so lacks the internal connection philosophical texts demand, being about their readers *as* readers. So philosophy is literature in that among its truth-conditions are those connected with being read, and reading those texts is supposed then to reveal us for what we are in virtue of our reading. Really to reveal us, however, not metaphorically, which is why, I think, I cannot finally acquiesce in the thought that philosophy is literature. It continues to aim at truth, but when false, seriously false, it is often also so fascinatingly false as to retain a kind of perpetual vitality as a metaphor. It is this which makes our history so impossible to relinquish, since the power is always there, and the texts engage us when we read them vitally as readers whose philosophical portraits materialize about us as we enter that place that awaited us from the beginning.

VIII.

Philosophizing Literature

Donald Barthelme invited me to address the graduate students of the writing program at the University of Houston on the topic of philosophy and literature. It struck me as an ideal opportunity to present the inverse of Essay VII. That essay seeks to argue that philosophy is not literature. This one seeks to argue that literature is not philosophy either. But the criterion I set forth for literature does mark out a special class of philosophical texts as having a literary dimension, namely those that embody as well as represent an idea. The present essay is not literature, by that criterion, however literary in manner it may be—after all, it was presented to a group of writers, and I was anxious not to be stodgy and— well—philosophical.

NOT SO TERRIBLY many years ago, the latest thought on the relationship between philosophy and art would have been found, typically if more stridently expressed than elsewhere, in the writings of Rudolph Carnap, a leader of the Logical Positivist school of philosophical analysis. Carnap wrote: "Many linguistic utterances are analogous to laughing, in that they have only an expressive function, no representative function. Examples are cries like 'Oh, Oh!' or, on a higher level, lyrical verse. Metaphysical propositions are . . . like laughing, lyrics, and music, expressive." By "metaphysical proposition" Carnap would have had in mind what anyone else would have in mind by "philosophy," much as he has in mind by "lyrical verse" any literary work to speak of: even coarse distinctions from this panoramic outlook are too fine to bother drawing, and there is a certain stammering grandeur in the manner with which in scarcely three sentences Carnap casts into the limbo of incoherence the sonnets of Shakespeare and *The World as Will and Idea,* understood as sophisticated giggles and winces, roundabout ways of venting feeling. The fulcrum by which all this civilized symptomology is to be levered out of the plane of discourse with a "representative function" was a principle of meaningfulness believed by Carnap and his cohorts to define the discourses of true cognition, namely scientific descriptions of the world. This was the celebrated and feared Verifiability Criterion of Meaningfulness, according to which an expression is meaningful only in case verifiable, at least in principle, through sense experience. It is a mark of how dominating this criterion was that it should have been regarded as a major daring amplification to suggest, as Karl Popper did, that *falsifiability* has a role to play in the sense of theories, but in any case laughing, lyrics, and metaphysics are lumped together and cut adrift by their ludicrous incapacity to survive what the Postivists supposed was a ludicrously weak test.

Then, in a gesture of what must have appeared stupifying generosity, performed perhaps in deference to Carnap's unregenerate and quite irrational love of poetry, these debased utterances were redeemed through acknowledgment of a secondary kind of meaning, identified by the Positivists as *emotive* meaning. This kind of meaning they supposed were shared, incidentally, by moral utterances as a class, which again but expressed the feelings of their voicers. All that poetry and philosophy carry by way of cognitive content is the evidence they provide, as symptoms, of the pathologies of those who write them. So far as glimpses, let alone deep glimpses into any ulterior reality, they are as null as loon cries echoing through the limberlost.

It is common knowledge that the subsequent history of the Verifiability Criterion has been very sad, offering a metaphor, almost, for geriatric medicine, where increasingly complex technologies are enlisted to prolong life by external, artificial means: the poor principle was wheeled from therapist to therapist, none of whom was able to staunch its chronic hemorrhages, since what it impugned as nonsense and what it admired as paradigmatically significant kept leaking into one another, and no way was ever finally found to preserve the sharp boundaries Carnap thought could be drawn between science and silliness. The logician Richard Jeffreys once said to me that the Verifiability Criterion was like the Sibyl of Cumea as described by Petronius and cited on the face page of *The Wasteland*: it wanted simply to die. No more than the Sibyl was it allowed a death with dignity, and it is my view that it continues to haunt the philosophical unconscious of contemporary thought to such a degree that if we were patiently to remove the disguises of current argument we would discern, at last, as basic pathogen, Verificationism's unquiet spirit. Verificationism, indeed, is itself but a disguise of one of the deep philosophical options it ironically sought to kill, namely philosophical idealism, whose masks are legion and whose essence is perhaps inextricable from thought. But that is a different story or kind of story from the one I am anxious to tell.

My aim is summoning the spirit is not to undertake that sort of structural diagnostic but to display it as a chapter in the long unedifying relationship between philosophy and art which begins in Plato: an enmity so deep that philosophy will not hesitate to consign to the ward of nonsense the whole of poetry even if at the cost of consigning a good bit of itself to that very ward. One need but place Aristophanes's portrait of the philosopher (in *The Clouds*) alongside Plato's portrait of the poet (in *The Republic*) to see the beginning of our interlocked destinies in western consciousness. I have argued in "The Philosophical Disenfranchisement of Art" that it is possible to view the entirety of platonic metaphysics as a cosmic labyrinth designed to keep art, like a minotaur, in logical quarantine, and possible as well to read the entire subsequent history of western aesthetics in much the same discreditable light: how else are we to understand the virtual consensus that the essence of art is its ephemerality, outside the framework of use and purpose which defines human life, something to be contemplated through the bars of the museum or the theater, at an irreducible distance from the world that really matters? There is a delicious justice in Carnap's suggestion that Plato himself, that crafty designer of a prison house for art, in fact is one of its inmates, since the theory of Forms belongs to the same family of utterances as the lyrics of Archilocus: it but expresses the feelings of the philosopher (= hatred of poetry): he might as well have written verse. "Metaphysics is a substitute, albeit an inadequate one, for art," Carnap wrote at the end of another essay, his thought being that metaphysicians use the *forms* of meaningful discourse (science) to create the illusion of meaning when it is in fact only the philosopher's feelings that are being expressed *en travestie*, and for which the structures of literature would be more suitable and less misleading. Carnap has in this regard special praise for Nietzsche. *Thus Spake Zarathustra* has an honesty not typically found in philosophical writing, since Nietzsche "does not choose the misleading theoretical form, but openly the form of art, of poetry."

There is a touch of inadvertent poetry in Carnap's portrait, as well as a touch of malice, and as with any caricature it wounds by exaggeration. The cartoon of the philosopher as a poet in a lab coat is unjust in the first instance to poetry, construed as nonsense not disguised as something else but wearing instead the vestments of its cognitive vacuity openly, like a fool in motley overalls. But in the second instance it is unjust to the profusion of philosophical forms, including that curious incantatory form Nietzsche chose in *Zarathustra*, a book which raises for the interpreter as many complex questions of narrational voice as *Remembrance of Things Past* does, and where ambiguity of voice—is it Nietzsche speaking or Zarathustra—refracts the message polyphonically in a way it is impossible to believe Nietzsche believed unconnected with a content it is also impossible to believe he could have believed, in principle, to be lacking. The array of philosophical forms is the richest I think there is, including of course the form of the scientific report favored by Carnap and his collaborators who, if anyone, selected the paraphernalia of objectivity and disinterestedness rhetorically conveyed by that form. Part of the reason, I am certain, that Logical Positivism was so threatening in its season was that it set forth its "findings" in papers suitable in format for the report, say, of spectroscopic operations on a given molecule, bristling with displayed formulae and the aggressive use of the new logical notations. If there is anywhere a set of writings in which feelings—hatred, scorn, contempt, perhaps fear, almost certainly hysteria—are expressed in the "misleading theoretical form," it the classical papers of the Vienna Circle. They are specimens of disciplined aggressivity. The "final solution to the problems of metaphysics" sounds an uncomfortable echo to other final solutions being noised about in the German-speaking world in the thirties and early forties.

Carnap's is but one of a class of responses to what we might term the Problem of Philosophy, which is the question of what philosophy is. Philosophy in the twentieth century may be exactly defined by the kind of problem it has become for itself—it is almost exactly what Heidegger supposed being human is, if man is that being for whom the nature of his being is in question: its being has just become that question. And two main kinds of responses have been evoked, both of which agree to the extent of rejecting the vast kind of claims made on their behalf by philosophy in ages of less self-doubt. One kind of response seeks to identify philosophy with the execution of some quite limited intellectual task, presented as what after all and stripped of excrescence is what philosophy always has essentially been. In the 1950s at Oxford, for example, philosophy was reduced to the canvass of ordinary usage, of what we say when; in the 1970s, in California, philosophy was more technically construed as the articulation of a semantics for natural languages. For Carnap philosophy set out to construct a formal language for science. The other response is more radical: it is in effect to nullify philosophy as the illusion of intellectual competence, an inert travesty of the labor of the mind—something that begins, as Wittgenstein said, only when language goes on holiday. And for me it is striking that no more compelling insultation has recommended itself than the lately widely endorsed thought of Derrida: that philosophy is but metaphor and that the texts of philosophy ought to be approached only as a genre of literature. One cannot have a very exalted view of literature if it is an act of deconstructive humiliation to assimilate philosophy to it: how high a view of women can we have if "feminine" is insulting when applied to men?

But deconstructive literary theory does not hold an especially high regard for literature either, compounding the intended degradation of philosophy, since its aim is to exalt criticism at the expense of both. Consider, since the analogy in any case is irresistible, the transformation into mere textual objects of literary works which parallels the reduction to mere sexual objects of women. To construe works of literature as mere objects, to be awakened to life by grammatological intervention, is to treat them as logically passive and existing for the interpretive pleasures of the hermeneutician. It is as though they were only for the critic, who knows how to keep them in their place, and hence is an aggression which takes its structures from sexual domination. The uncadenced enthusiasm with which deconstruction has been accepted by members of the literary establishment must suggest a sense of emancipation from texts which heretofore had promised a meaning to be discovered by hard intellectual work, but now stand as infinitely pliant to whatever meaning one cares to impose. So we find in metacriticism today a reenactment of the conflict between theory and literature with which philosophy began its long and latterly unedifying career. Philosophy began by defining itself through the suppression of poetry: so there is a dialectical irony in the fact that philosophical texts have come to be pitched together in with literary texts, subject now to a common degradation.

Well, if philosophy is that close to literature that they can by mutual enemies be treated as one, it might begin to reachieve the dignity it sought at the expense of literature by undertaking the redignification of literature itself. And then it may examine itself to see whether it indeed has the dignity it finds in art. My sense of the matter is that it does not have *that* dignity, but a dignity of its own that only can be claimed by distinguishing it from that of art. The philosopher of art today has the task of a double reenfranchisement, with one reenfranchisement being a condition for the other. I find in this a final irony, namely that the destiny of its own identity should be complicated with what philosophers, characteristically of their scorn for art, should have dismissed as philosophy's most peripheral, almost frivolous branch. On my view the philosophy of art is the *heart* of philosophy.

By a curious internal evolution in the art of our own century, philosophy has virtually been handed a certificate of authenticity by its ancient enemy, in the sense that the definition of art has been demonstrated to be a philosophical problem, from which it follows that so long as art exists there has to be a place for philosophy as well. By this I mean that art has shown that the class of artworks does not constitute a natural kind, so that the distinction between works of art and other things is not finally a matter of science. This has been shown through the emergence of works of art which cannot be told apart from mere objects which are not works of art, though the two resemble one another in every perceptual particular. This was achieved preeminently by Duchamp, and then brilliantly extended and exploited in the 1960s by Warhol, Lichtenstein, Oldenburg, and others. Take any of Duchamp's readymades, say the bottle rack, counterparts to which could still be purchased not many years ago in the *quincailleries* of France: perhaps they still are to be found. Now bottle racks constitute a natural kind in that they share the set of properties that go with being a bottle rack, and which you can check out against the standard criteria. But here, in no respect different from its peers, is a bottle rack by those criteria—but it is also a work of art, with a title, pedigree, date of execution, and as pricey as truffles. Now Duchamp did a number of readymades, and could have done any number, and it is easy to imagine that he did them from can openers, snowplows, balloon pumps, instead of bicycle wheels, grooming combs, and urinals. So any natural kind can have yielded up a work of art as indiscernible from its peers as the bottle rack is from its peers. But this heterogeneous set of objects can have no very interesting properties in common; they have in common, in fact, whatever members of all the natural kinds have in common, which may not be much. But all are works of art, or can be.

Consider what scientists call isomers: molecules composed of the same elements united in the same proportion by weight, hence indiscernible in point of composition and size. They nevertheless have different properties and so there must be some internal difference which accounts for it, and this turns out to be a difference in structure, in the way the same elements are connected up. Thus urea and ammonium cyanate are represented by the same formula, CON_2H_4. They differ chemically, however, and this is explained through their structures. Now it is impossible to suppose that Duchamp's bottle rack differs from just the routine bottle rack in anything like the way a pair of isomers differ, or that careful scientific analysis of it will demonstrate wherein the difference lies. And since the class of artworks does not constitute a natural kind, it is difficult to suppose that the analysis of art is to be resolved by scientific means. But the problem presented by the readymades is precisely of the form of all philosophical problems.

Philosophical problems arise whenever we have indiscernibles belonging as it were to different philosophical kinds: where there is a difference but not a natural one. The paradigm of a philosophical difference is between two worlds, one of which is sheer illusion, as the Indians believed this one is, and the other of which is real in the way *we* believe this very world is. Descartes's problem of distinguishing waking experience from dream experience is a limited variation of the same question, where it is clear that nothing internal to the experience is going to effect the differentiation. Other exemplars are readily furnished. A world of sheer determinism might be imagined indistinguishable from one in which everything happens by accident. A world in which God exists could never be told apart from one in which God didn't, since God is not one of the things in the world, as might in a primitive religion like that of the Old Testament have been supposed. When confronted with two worlds exactly alike one of which is suffused with the invisible presence of God—if God were visible, the problem would not be philosophical—James said choose the world that makes a difference. Carnap would have said that such a choice is meaningless precisely because no observation(s) could be summoned to effect a discrimination. Hume sought to analyze laws in terms of habits of expectation and would insist then that the world of determinism and the world of sheer accident are the same in that nothing more can be offered than these habits to differentiate them: anything further, in his idiom, would be a "distinction without a difference." Whatever the case, it is plain that philosophical differences are external to the worlds they discriminate, and, in a lesser, more tractable way, this is the case with works of art that are not to be told apart from real objects that otherwise perfectly resemble them.

It is this latter problem that has been made vivid in our century, since before it had seemed as if artworks did constitute a natural kind, even one identifiable on perceptual grounds. Art revealed its philosophical nature when it became plain that though the differences were immense be-

tween the *Brillo Box* of the Warhol and the mere container for
soap pads, they could not be identified or explained by anything like a scientific analysis. It required rather a philosophical analysis, and I credit myself with having carried out the
preliminary stages of one in *The Transfiguration of the Commonplace*. I do not mean to rehearse the itinerary of that book
here, but only to underline its method, which is to try,
whenever you think there is a philosophical distinction to be
made, to manufacture a pair of indiscernibilia belonging to
what you suppose are distinct philosophical kinds and then
say in what the difference consists—and then to apply this
method to the present case.

So let us raise the possibility of a pair of texts, one philosophy and one literature, which might be as indiscernible
as required so that we are not to distinguish them by any
surface characteristic. (It was exactly by borrowing the surface characteristics of the scientific report that Carnap sought
to confer cognitive respectability on what were in the end
philosophical texts masked, as many are, as attacks on philosophy.) *Nausea*, a novel by a philosopher, has the form of a
journal, while *Journal métaphysique*, by Gabriel Marcel—a
dramatist as well as philosopher—is a philosophical work in
the form of a journal: so they pair off as to form. Both contain philosophical thoughts, but containing philosophical
thoughts won't make something into a philosophical text, or
certain fortune cookies that have come my way would
qualify. *Nausea* is not a philosophical text, *Journal Métaphysique* is. Defoe's *Journal of the Plague Year* is a novel in the form
of a journal, but Defoe was no philosopher at all, however
philosophically interesting Crusoe is: and though about
death and dying, heavy subjects indeed, is itself, as a book,
not even remotely philosophical. Pepys's *Diaries* are a journal
without being either a novel or philosophical. So we cover
all bases, exhaustively: a journal which is philosophical
without being a novel, a journal which is a novel and might
be philosophical, a journal which is a novel without being
philosophical, and a journal which is neither a novel nor a

piece of philosophy. All of these have considerable differences, one from another: they are not as similar as *Brillo Box*
and the boxes of Brillo: but they serve collective notice that
however we effect our differentiation, it is not going to be on
the basis of checking out form and content. Even Pepys may
have a stray philosophical thought, and I should hate to be
stuck with a differentiation based on counting: and I am
convinced that what makes a work philosophical is not a
matter of frequency of philosophical thoughts. A dictionary
of philosophical quotations would contain more of these
than the *Metaphysics* of Aristotle.

One last point before proceeding to cases. I have often
maintained that philosophical questions always can be given
a form which makes possible a strategy of juxtaposing indiscriminable counterparts. This means that the task of differentiating philosophy from literature is an internal question
of philosophy, a question that cannot be answered without
saying in part what philosophy is. It is at best an external
question for literature, something writers may or may not be
concerned with. That it is an internal question of philosophy
can be seen from the fact that there is an unbroken line of
philosophers from Plato to Carnap whose philosophy is defined through seeking just this differentiation. Plato after all
wrote dialogues, and perhaps he had the urgent sense that
something had to differentiate these from dramas. Though
traditionally it was an external question of literature—it cannot have been a problem for writers to differentiate themselves from philosophy in part because they often aspired to
philosophy—it has in our time become an urgent question
for art, literature included. It has become this because of art
having come so close to becoming its own philosophy that it
seemed to require a rescue by philosophy in order that art
should not lose its identity in philosophical reflection upon
itself. Literature might simply have turned into philosophy in
an act of self-transcending—which is still enough different
from philosophy turning into literature, or being discovered
to have been literature all along, according to such claims as

Carnap's or Derrida's, that some basis for this felt difference remains to articulate. In the remainder of this essay I shall begin this articulation.

I want to distinguish the texts of literature from the texts which are not literature, supposing that differences in being *literary* count for nothing much either way. A certain amount of philosophy may be more literary than some literature, that is to say, and this does not seem to me a deep difference. Santayana wrote philosophy in a literary way and he also produced a wonderful novel, but he would have been uncomfortable if the literary properties of his philosophical prose caused *Skepticism and Animal Faith* to be lumped together with *The Last Puritan* as literature. It would also be useful to dismiss as irrelevant the rather more common criterion that sunders fact from fiction. It is perfectly possible for fiction to be false—for instance, in the sense of containing false statements—and in my own case I find it disfiguring when I encounter it. A friend begins a novel with some people driving *up* Fifth Avenue, a southbound-only street, and I could not read further: a man whose grip on reality is that weak is not necessarily to be trusted with the more delicate psychic facts to which we expect a novelist to be true.

A worse case is a story in a recent *New Yorker* by Cynthia Ozick, in any case psychologically far-fetched, which may be the price of reading Ozick at all. If her characters read the world wrong, well, that is the sort of thing at which she perhaps aims—but then one has to have confidence that *she* reads the world right. This story takes place in Italy in the Fascist era, and she goes to some pains to get her readers clear on the historical locus of her improbable love story. The last segment takes place in Milan, where a certain statue plays a crucial symbolic role. This is the *Rondanini Pietà* of Michelangelo, in actual fact located in a beautiful museum in Milan's Castello Sforzesco, where Ozick's lovers wander hand-in-hand. They could wander there today but not in the period she sets her story in, for there was no such museum then and the *Rondanini* was until 1953 in the possession of the San Sèverino family in Rome. I was considerably more upset by this than by the after all rather benign fabrications of Alasdaire Read, of which so much was made when they were revealed, sanctimonious editorials in the *New York Times* saying that there is a name for what Read was doing, namely fiction. But falsehood has no place in fiction either, and I vastly prefer plausible figures in the true world than implausible figures in a world which means to be true but is false. At the end of *Dale Loves Sophie to Death*, Robb Forman Dew has the husband muse about a saying of Mies van der Rohe: "God is in the details." This is a saying of Flaubert; Mies said, "Less is more," and it is quite exact that the wimp should get such things wrong, even more exact since he is a teacher of literature, and while there is a lingering suspicion that Robb Forman Dew herself may have gotten it wrong, there is room for a possible credit to irony, whereas nothing mitigates Ozick's lapse (I would have hated her story even if I did not have this particular reason—or excuse—for hating it). Whatever the case, truth and falsity will not especially enter my analysis.

Let us ponder, then, a pair of isomeric texts, texts characterized by the same elements united in the same proportion by weight, but where they differ in their properties—one is literature and the other not—and so we seek an explanatory difference, following the imperatives of organic chemistry, in their structures. And just to apply the maximum pressure, let us suppose them identical in so many respects that such residual differences as may persist cannot seriously be supposed to account for the presence or absense of the property. Thus our texts are to be considerably closer than, say, *Hamlet* is to the story of Amletus in Saxo Grammaticus's *Historia Danica*, though nothing could be more "literary" than the latter, cast as it is in euphuistic Latin verse, and the former is after all disfigured by a ghost in the *dramatis personae*: Marcellus, Bernardo, and Horatio see it, so it is not merely a projection of the sick imagination of the brooding prince. So let's imagine that there really was a village once in which a weaver led a lonely life, turned miser because of his loneliness, was robbed by a local lordling—the ne'er-do-well brother of the real father of a foundling who crawls into the weaver's house by lucky accident. And she, that very foundling, despite aristocratic genes—or blood, as they would have said at the time—marries a local lad named Ronnie in real life, though Aaron in George Eliot's novel. We learn all this from a text with a certain amount of literary merit, but in fact simply a rather rambling piece of parish history, set down by a forgotten archivist in Raveloe who could not resist moral asides. The other is a work of literature, one of those works indeed by which the meaning of the word "literature" is taught to agonized and resistant high school students throughout the land. It would not bother me that *Silas Marner* were "based on" the chronicle even more closely than Hamlet is based on the story of Amletus: it would not even bother me that the texts are so close that the whisper of plagiarism spontaneously arises: changing "Aaron" for "Ronnie" could neither get George Eliot (small wonder she would not write under her own name!) off the hook, or account for the claim that hers is literature while the text written by a man whose *real name is* George Elliott—two *l*'s, two *t*'s—is not. Where's the justice, but more important, what's the argument?

George Eliot (one *l*, one *t*) gives us I think a cue in a letter written to her friend Frederick Harrison in 1866—five years after the publication of *Silas Marner.*

That is a tremendously difficult problem; its difficulties press upon me, who have gone through again and again the severe effort of trying to make certain ideas thoroughly incarnate, as if they had revealed themselves to me first in the flesh and not in the spirit. I think aesthetic teaching the highest of all teaching because it deals with life in its highest complexity. But if it ceases to be purely aesthetic—if it lapses anywhere from the picture to the diagram— it becomes the most offensive of all teaching.

By "aesthetic teaching" Eliot means: teaching through a work of art, of the sort *Silas Marner* is meant to exemplify, rather than teaching the same point, by means perhaps of a sermon or a lecture, that her text aims to teach aesthetically. The sermon or lecture would stand to her text as diagram to picture, I suppose, to use her stunning contrast. Of course we today have come to appreciate that there are pictures which are indistinguishable from diagrams but "teach" even so in very different ways: Roy Lichtenstein's *Portrait of Madame Cézanne* is photographically so similar to a diagram in Erle Lorans book *Cézanne's Composition* that the author of the latter sued the painter of the former for plagiarism: yet the diagram merely shows us a composition while the painting points the way into the heart of the artist. And the artist Arakawa has done paintings which use the idiom of diagrams without being diagrams at all. Of course the same distinction is possible in the verbal medium as well: an early chapter of *The Adventures of Augie March* was, though enough of a story to be published as such in *Partisan Review,* really in the form of a sermon, as is a famous chapter in *Moby Dick.* In any case the distinction is absolute, I believe, and it seems to me that one difference between literature and philosophy, let alone literature and other sorts of texts such as parish histories, is enwrapped in this distinction.

The term "idea" of course is drawn from the inner lexicon of metaphysics, and I doubt that in Eliot's usage it has much to do with the psychological use of the term, or with authorial intention in any simple way: she is not making the standard complaint that it is difficult to transform one's thought into actual writing, to embody ideas, in that sense, in written words. There is that struggle, and all of us who write at all are familiar with it, but I do not believe it is that to which she refers. Ideas make their fateful entry into western theorizing in some famous passages in Plato, whose complaint against works of art was specifically that they do *not* embody ideas but only appear to. Ideas in his philosophy were the forms that actual objects in our world possess, and by possessing which achieve what degree of intelligibility, imperfect though it be, such objects may be said to have. Objects are appreciated as marginally translucent, enabling us to make out, dimly, the form or Ideas with which they are irradiated, as though through a glass darkly. St. Paul, like Plato, envisioned the possibility of direct cognitive encounters with such forms when we leave behind the impediments of sense and subsist as beings of pure intellect. But as it stands, the world we inhabit is a fusion of the eternal and the temporal, literally so in that mongrel of Greek and Jewish theory, Christianity, where God takes on human form and enters history as the word made suffering flesh.

Silas Marner is idea made flesh in George Eliot's literary metaphysics, and she enunciates, in my view, an impeccable philosophy of art. What makes *Brillo Box* a work of art is that it incarnates, expresses, whatever idea it does express, hence is idea and mere thing at once, a box transfigured if only into the idea of a box. The Brillo boxes of routine use in the shipping and storage of soap pads incarnates no such idea, though of course Plato would suppose they must, just to be intelligible as boxes at all, whereas we might simply suppose they satisfy the criteria of cartonhood and incarnate nothing at all. It goes without saying, of course, that it is specifically such things as ideas that Carnap supposes the Verifiability Criterion is going to vaporize into nonsense, but it is unclear that even today we have any clear way of doing without them or something like them, since they remain a part of philosophical discourse under the name of meaning. Frege, only for instance, found it necessary to posit a realm of thoughts for expressions to mean, since it was plain to Frege that something like the thought was needed to explain the fact that two expressions might stand for the same thing and yet differ in meaning: he would say they present different thoughts—though by "thoughts" he meant nothing psychological, and though he supposed, mysteriously, that to understand an expression is to grasp the thought it expresses. It is mysterious because thoughts, as he construed them, are mysterious, occupying a third world, neither mental nor material. But something like Frege's structure seems irresistible in the present context. Our parish history refers to an actual weaver in an actual town, to a real foundling and her true husband when she grows to womanhood. In that sense of reference, *Silas Marner* may refer to nothing, being a work of fiction. In point of semantical theory, we may understand the one as we understand the other, by "grasping the thoughts" the words express, if that is what we do and if there were the faintest possibility that there are thoughts in Frege's sense. But beyond that *Silas Marner* incarnates an idea the grasping of which is different from what understanding may be involved in the understanding of words, which *Silas Marner* shares with its counterpart or isomer in village history. I find myself wanting to think of *Brillo Box* as possessing a kind of soul, admittedly imperceptible since its counterparts, lacking souls, look exactly like it. The character of Silas Marner too may, in the medium of the novel *Silas Marner*, incarnate a dimension of significance the person referred to in the parish narrative lacks. Let me try to clarify what these admittedly obscure suggestions might mean, and hence why the idiom of incarnating an idea is so appealing.

Suppose there really was, as the narrative holds, this weaver in this village, who lost his gold by theft but gained a truer gold by fate, and in the process was taken up and supported by the simple folk of the village who up to then had found him strange and alien, a kind of male witch. Imagine that the writer of the narrative gives it to him to check up against his recollections, and he vouches for its accuracy: Yep, that's just the way it was. Effie crept in by the fire. Why if I hadn't kept the door open, looking for something, the poor dear would have froze to death . . . and so, garrulously, on. Now suppose the manuscript comes to the attention of George Eliot herself, who sees in it not just that set of events but something universal, a parable of love and meaning, the incarnation of an idea about the sweet and bitter of existence. And she publishes it as the novel *Silas*

Marner, which Silas Marner, if that was his name, reads in a
very different spirit than he read the narrative, and if it works
as she intended he will suddenly not only grasp the thought
incarnate in the text, but will see his own life in the light of
that thought, will see his life as written there as a metaphor
for his life as actually led. He sees that it is about him in a
very different way than the parish history was. But in the
way it is about him as a novel, it is about *whoever* reads it,
providing the same metaphor for the life of every reader. A
Jew whose life is led among upperclass wasps might in this
sense find that he *is,* not literally but by virtue of metaphoric
transformation, Charles Swann: but you don't have to be
Jewish for *Swann's Way* to be about you either. Silas Marner
is Silas Marner in the straight path of reference, but Silas
Marner is also *Silas Marner* in the different path of metaphorical identification. But Silas Marner is any of us in that
way as well. The novel teaches aesthetically in that it gives
the reader's life the meaning that the book incarnates. This is
what it seems to me that George Eliot (one *l,* one *t*) achieved
that George Elliott (two of each) does not, even though their
texts might be perfect isomers. There even is a sense, which I
shall not develop here, in which *Brillo Box* is about the
viewer of it—I leave it as an exercise for the reader to figure
out how.

    I have been deploying a certain number of fictional
strategies—the imaginery example as *Dankenexperiment* is
standard philosophical praxis—in order to begin to construct
a diagram, in George Eliot's sense, of her philosophy of literature. Her novels certainly conform to her theory, some more
than others, in that each seeks to embody an idea it is the
task of the reader to grasp: reading in such a case is more
than understanding the words (grasping the thoughts they
mean, in Frege's semantical account), more even than understanding the thought the text may express, if this should be
different from what the words as such mean: it is grasping

the thought the text *embodies* and which the characters, in themselves and in their relationships, incarnate. The flesh of incarnation is finer in the case of Eliot than in Dickens, whose characters are walking ideas with no identity beyond that, but the question I want to raise is this: do her novels, in addition to conforming to her philosophy, *embody* the idea her philosophy requires? Do they embody the idea of embodiment, or do they only illustrate it? Perhaps only a philosopher would put the question this way, but embodiment, as I have sought to make plain, is a philosophical idea of some weight and lineage, is perhaps the idea that got philosophy going in the West, and if *Silas Marner*—or any novel—embodied or incarnated that idea, well, it would embody a philosophical idea while remaining literature, and so have its cake and eat it too. I cannot suppose that just in virtue of embodying an idea, a novel or poem embodies the idea of embodiment—for then every work of literary art would embody the same idea and each would in effect embody the philosophy of literature—teach the idea of literature aesthetically. Of course embodiment is not the only philosophical idea, but we at least can say what a novel must do in order to be, in addition to literature, a work of philosophical literature: it must embody a philosophical idea. Each such work would have, in a way, to be a metaphor for itself. All works would be philosophical, on the other hand, if each embodied the idea of embodiment: and this seems to me too prodigal. There are novels that seek to embody the idea of the novel, and if that is the idea of embodiment, then these novels embody that idea: but this is a special class of highly self-reflexive works, these days more frequently encountered than in Eliot's time. It may be a definition of modernity that the modern novel is philosophical in this way.

If the embodiment of ideas is the mark of literature, and if the embodiment of philosophical ideas is the mark of philosophical literature, well I suppose a certain subclass of philosophical texts must be examples of philosophical literature in this sense, inasmuch as they embody what they are about.

Someone might argue that every argument embodies the
idea of argument, or that every philosophical text embodies
the idea of philosophy, whatever the argument may have as
conclusion or the text as primary subject: but if literature is
the embodiment of ideas, every philosophical text would
then be literature, and I find this too wholesale: and it may
blur the line between exemplification and embodiment it
ought to be imperative for a philosophy of literature to keep
apart. But there are philosophical texts which embody much
in the way in which, I suppose, *Silas Marner* does. The early
dialogues of Plato are good cases: *Lysis* is about friendship,
but it embodies what it is about in the relationship between
Socrates and the youth he engages in conversation: that is
what friendship *is*, so you have an example of what the dialogue abstractly discusses. The *Meno* embodies the idea of
recollection in having the slave boy produce a proof of a
theorem he cannot have learned in this life. *The Symposium*
certainly embodies its subject, which is love, in the wild
frenzied interruption by the drunken Alcibiades of the feast
of reason in which the feeling up to then was only discussed:
the contrast between feeling and thought could not be more
dramatically shown. *The Republic* embodies the rational construction through rational discourse of the foundations of a
just society, and demonstrates how reason can dominate
force in the marvelous exchange of the thesis that might is
right by Thrasymachus and Socrates. The *Meditations* of
Descartes embodies the search for clear and distinct ideas it
also describes, and it is a book that cannot be read as books
are usually read: one must engage in the search oneself, and
in the end be transformed into a living instance of what the
text recommends. John Dewey's *Logic: The Theory of Inquiry*
shows what it also describes and so becomes, by this criterion, an unlikely work of art. Just possibly Locke's *Essay
Concerning Human Understanding* puts in our hands exactly
what it talks about, like a book about books: it *is* the abstract
concept of understanding verbally embodied.

But some ideas may be too abstract for embodiment, so

that the texts addressing these are best when as transparent as possible, contributing nothing of their own to the intellectual grasp of their topics. And this may be true of the platonic corpus as well. Friendship, love, justice: these are things about which we have strong intuitions and whose instances we may recognize even when the concepts elude our definitional powers. Sometimes, just because of this, when one has novel views of love, friendship, and justice, one has to show that they are possible: and setting an example before us is a powerful demonstration. But when Plato set forth into unknown waters, as in the *Timaeus* or the *Sophist*, the relationship to common intuition was very tenuous, and I tend to think the dialogic paradigm less and less adequate: there are a limited number of things that dialogue, even when amply conceived, is capable of embodying.

But I think this generally true as philosophical inquiry advances. Of course there are programs in philosophy where the connections to intuition must be strong. Phenomenology, as the analysis of the structures of consciousness and hence of the intuition of essences, as Husserl describes this, must count finally on the reader's own colloboration: in some way what those texts analyze must materialize within the reader's consciousness or they cannot be right. Ordinary language philosophy had in the end to count on the reader's lexical intuitions and the texts had to embody their insights. I think the *Logical Investigations* of Wittgenstein embody the clarifications the text addresses through the comfortable little interchanges between the writer and *Du*—perhaps himself—and one internalizes this text as one must the *Meditations*. But there are vast areas of philosophy where there are no intuitions or where they conflict with one another: or where the authority of intuition is itself in issue so that embodiment would beg the question. This is surprisingly the case in what must seem to lie closest to us of all possible things, the human mind.

Nor is it at all necessarily an enhancement of philosophy, outside some of the programs I have sketched, that it should aspire to the status of literature. I happen to take special pains with writing, I think not common in my profession, and I was naturally pleased when critics said, of my *Transfiguration of the Commonplace*, that it was what it set out to analyze, a work of art in its own right, so that I at least could be said to know what art is even if my analysis was wrong—another case of intuition outstripping the writer's powers of analysis. But the compliment, it seems to me, confuses literary quality with literature. I don't have the patience to embody my ideas, and I am uncertain the understanding of my writing would be enhanced if I could, say, incarnate them in a novel. As a philosopher I want to mainline, to get directly to the issue. Other philosophers differ: it is difficult to think of William Gass, for instance, as mainlining, but his subject, often, is words and writing and reading, so he is able to make his points by putting his readers through an experience of the sort he has set out to analyze. In point of analysis, he could probably say in three pages what he uses thirty pages to pursue: but the pursuit is part of what he wants. But neither can it be an accident that he is a novelist, for whom embodiment means something it cannot embody for me.

Now I think the connection between literature and intuition much narrower than it is between intuition and philosophy, and especially so if literature means to be edifying and educational, as Eliot meant it to be. If it is to be educational, for instance, the reader falls within the subjects it treats of, and the text must be about him. And if that sort of metaphoric identification is to be possible, where Silas Marner can say, "I am Silas Marner" or I "I am Charles Swann," or Cézanne say, "I am Frenhofer," alluding to the dubious hero of Balzac's *Chef d'oeuvre inconnu*—then literature cannot stray very far from the structures that define the life of those who read novels: love, jealousy, friendship, adventure, conflict and crisis, the tight corner of the human soul, death, family, childhood, memory, betrayal and loss, sacrifice, happy endings, romance, duty, and meaning. And sex and work and ideals. Now I can see an artist growing restless with these constraints, wanting to slip free of the common experience, not in the sense of writing about sex in distant galaxies, where we inevitably carry with us the values and preferences and possibilities of our own dear planet, but in wanting to be philosophical about what after all defines one as an artist—writing, say. A lot of contemporary literature aims at that.

And it achieves its aims in embodying ideas about writing, but in so doing it addresses its readers as readers, and not as men and women with the sorts of problems and questions the great writers took as the essence of their art. It is as though the reader were addressed as one reduced to the competences involved in the structuring or destructuring of texts, and as though the texts were about nothing much but themselves, and the boundaries of the library or the classroom become the boundaries of life. When this happens, the reductions of contemporary literary theory have been anticipated. The boundary between literature and theory, perhaps between literature and philosophy, will have been erased. And if there is nothing outside the text, well, living is a form of reading.

Eliot believed the boundary to be indelible. To Lady Ponsonby she wrote: "Consider what the human mind en masse would have been had there been no such combination of elements in it as has produced poets. All the philosophers and savants would not have sufficed to supply that deficiency. And how can the life of nations be understood without the inward life of poetry?—that is of emotion blending with thought?" In a way, I suppose, the texts of contemporary criticism offer a picture of what the human mind en masse would be if literature were reduced to so many textual specimens, and readers reduced to theorists of reading, and life reduced to literature in such a way that the diagram becomes the picture.

Meanwhile, I cannot forebear observing the chemical vocabulary in this singular passage. The "combination of elements" which makes for poetry suggests that a different combination might make for philosophy, so that we are isomers of one another and satisfy a common formula closely enough that on a shallow reading, philosophy might be perceived as literature if literature is perceived simply as texts, and hence as subjects for literary theory. I have sought in this paper to outline a deeper view, based on the intuition that poetry and philosophy have properties too finally different to be forms of one another's elements. But the true chemistry of the subject awaits its Daltons, its Wohlers, its Kekules.

IX.

Art, Evolution, and the Consciousness of History

Presented to the American Society for Aesthetics at Louisville, Kentucky, at the invitation of Mary Wiseman, this was the fourth Mandel Lecture. David Mandel endowed a lecture, to be given every other year, on some aspect of the relationship between evolution and art. Mr. Mandel has expressed the belief that "art plays the major role in furthering man's future evolution," and I decided, in accepting the invitation, to be good guest enough to address Mandel's views. It in any case enabled me to advance beyond "The End of Art" the views on the history of art there advanced, and to say something further on the relationship between art and philosophy.

WHO BUT THE father specifically of Leonardo da Vinci would have undertaken the grandiose project of replicating his astounding offspring by the agency of planned parenthood? Piero da Vinci, in an experiment in husbandry which demonstrates through its imaginative audacity that the great artificer was after all a chip off the old block, sought to recreate circumstances as similar to those under which Leonardo

was conceived as could be managed, in the confident extravagant hope that if woman, room, and astrological configu-
ration were all sufficiently similar, great expectations as to
similarity of issue must be in order. Piero's thought was that
genius was more likely to be genetic than the product of
education, though it cannot have hurt to have had Verocchio
as master—and a man that bent on reconstituting circumstance to a point of morphological indiscernibility would
hardly have been casual about the nurture of his scion. He
had the brilliant thought that breeding for genius was of a
piece with breeding for any desirable trait or set of traits, and
thus drew upon a kind of barnyard lore that was to give
Darwin his paradigm three centuries later. Piero cogently argued through his action that too little is known about the
causal determinants of genius to take anything for granted:
the mechanisms of selection are of a piece with those exploited in the production of pigeons of a certain shape or
coloration—Darwin's own case—but the chance of begetting
another Leonardo would have been too momentous to be
casual even about bedcloths and chamber pots. His was a
brilliant but in the end comically superstitious effort at what
would not have been called artificial selection at the time,
since there was no other kind of selection known about to
make the description meaningful. There are after all families
that breed for leanness, meanness, or looks, and in the sixteenth century the breeding bed was a place of power: it did
not escape the notice of the portraitists of those in power that
certain phenotypical features kept reappearing in the carefully interbred Hohenzollern or Hauenstauffen or Hapsburgs.
If a certain chin, a certain disposition to idiocy could be
counted on when like bred like, why not genius when very
like bred with very like? Piero simply aimed for very high
things.

The connotations of "higher" strike an ominous retroac-
tive overtone in the light of beings of a higher order specula-
ted about in the nineteenth century, after Darwin and on into
our own, climaxing, of course, in the dread racial premisses

of National Socialism. But there is little question but what The Artist—I use the capital letters of romantic typography— would have stood as one of the more benign exemplars of a higher order of humanity held up by prophets as the redemption of the species. Goethe and Michelangelo were instances Nietzsche offers of what he had in mind by *Der Übermensch*—he also mentions Cesare Borgi and Napoleon— and while Nietzsche supposed it a kind of sacred duty to make the *Übermensch* possible—I think he had too low a view of ordinary humans seriously to have advanced the imperative that *we* should be as much like the *Übermensch* as possible—he is not especially helpful as to how this is to be achieved. But by what mechanism other than artificial selection could it be achieved, supposing the attributes of *Übermenschlicheit* heritable? The transmission of musical traits in the Bach family showed that certain gifts were as capable of being passed on as eye color, obesity, or double-jointedness, if only those possessed of such gifts did not breed as randomly and irresponsibly as artists do, like the rest of us fixated on what Nietzsche might regard as quite incidental and irrelevant traits such as dimples, twinkles, salient bosoms, and curls. If the *Übermensch* is to redeem us, is it not perhaps even immoral to leave such matters to the mercy of random variation? It was inevitable that eugenic regimentation should seem an appropriate social program in the ghastly political era that begins with the publication, in 1859, of *The Origin of Species* with its fateful, I should say disastrous, subtitle, "Or the Preservation of Favored Races in the Struggle for Life." It is in the subtitle that Darwin displays his genius for a rhetoric that would assure the preservation of his ideas in their own struggle for survival. The language has the adaptive function of protecting the fragile theory until it achieves sufficient cognitive strength to survive on its own terms. That the idiom of struggle, preservation, favoredness, and race should have been a moral toxin we have yet to expel would have been a matter of as little interest to the tender infant theory as the fact that it is causing immense distress to

the woman carrying it does to the indifferent fetus. Its was
the struggles that his language caused that transferred attention away from beetles and goldfinch to humanity as a high
type and the artist as the highest human type, almost as if it
were a stunning diversionary tactic to enable the scientific
investigations his theories needed if they were to prevail to
be carried forward in peace. How provident if true, considering that quite advanced philosophers of science even today
dispute the scienticity of evolutionary theory as subtly as
others moot the legitimacy as science of psychoanalytical
theory. "There exists no law of evolution" wrote Sir Karl
Popper, and the scientific vincibility of evolutionism has
been, apart from the assurances of sacred writ, the chief
weapon of "Scientific Creationism" in advancing its claims
by reducing those of Darwinism to mere hypothesis, leaving
logical space for alternatives. Evolutionary theory is flourish-
ing today, but what price mankind has had to pay in terms of
holocausts for its domination chills the blood to contemplate. Well, the darwinians might say, it was never their posture to deny that it is a cruel and difficult arena in which the
struggle for life takes place: why should it be any different
with ideas, which have their own morphology, than with the
myriad other forms of life?

Rhetoric is never historically that isolable from the substance of theories that we cannot seriously ask whether the
theory might have occurred to its discoverer without the
rhetorical premisses that recommended it. Darwin's theory
certainly keeps company with creationsim in postulating
that which in effect anthropomorphizes to nature the breeding practices mimicked by Piero da Vinci: nature is the hus-
bandman writ large, selecting (Darwin's term) by natural
means in precise analogy to the way we select artificially,
and treating species as we treat varieties. Human breeders
have never had the power of breeding a new hereditary trait,
but only guiding, through judicious matching, what human
need or fancy initially selects out as desirable. Darwinism
supposes a deep analogy between barnyard and universe, as

between natural and artificial selection, so that it must have been irresistable to suppose a further analogy between the criteria used by nature for selecting traits and those husbandmen would cite: hence "the fittest" carries the sorts of connotations of desirability the breeder would invoke in making the case for wooliness in sheep or plump-breastedness in fowl. It would have been equally irresistible to a still essentially religious mentality not to see in natural selection something like the same operations of the Hidden Hand that was believed to guide, through the mechanisms of the market, human choices which finally lead to the best possible distribution of goods, with everyone possessed of what she or he wants in the highest quality at the most reasonable price. That there should be suffering along the way —the elimination of unfit species and the elimination of harmful traits in existing species, on the one hand; the elimination of the uncompetitive and the economically inferior on the other—would be just the cost, or kind of cost, that evolution toward a desired end state must be expected to exact; not costs at all if we take the long view with which the problem of evil has made us familiar down the ages. The pigeon breeder finds a use for culls in pigeon pies, saving the best for further breeding. Nature must aim at the sort of end state at which we aim, and though somewhat diffident in proclaiming this, Darwin believed human beings no less marvelous for having evolved as we would have been had we been immediately created by blowing life into a handful of dust. The prophets of the superman simply raised the ante, prizing varietally rare constellations of traits, say those exemplified in Leonardo; and saw no moral obstacle to breeding for these. If nature can bring forth man from lower primates, why can we not make ours a species of genius by breeding traits already present but so far too much a matter of chance? Leonardo himself seemed little inclined to the act upon which generation depended, which may be why Piero took matters in his own hands. The question is why we would want to breed for artistic talent?

Modern breeding practice discriminates between fancy and utility breeding, and it is an interesting speculation whether leonardi belong to the one class or the other. The fancy breed owes its existence to aesthetic preference: the long horn of cattle, the dished face and bowed legs of the bulldog, the pendulous ear of the basset hound, the lustrous hackles of the Nicobar pigeon: these are selected for the delectation of fanciers, utility be damned. It is the fancy breed that wins cups and ribbons at dog shows, and it is arguable that fanciness may entail inutility, in the respect that usefulness may be compromised by a hypertropied trait: the ratio of length to height in the dachshund was useful when the animals were bred for badger hunting, but it becomes counterfunctional when the ratio projects an ideal dachshund in which length approaches infinity as height approaches zero. It is just here that artificial nurture runs counter to nature, since such exaggerated ratios would not stand up against the exigencies of environment. Artists are notorious for their incapacity to cope in the struggle for existence, which suggests that nature would not especially favor their survival under the rigors of natural selection.

There is a long tradition that the artist belongs to the fanciful rather than the utilitarian variety of human, and the standard biographical myth approves of the composer or painter disqualified for normal existence in the pursuit of his or her art. We have come to expect a degree of eccentricity in our artists which we accept as the price for genius, with the consequence that we are suspicious of the artist capable of normal activities: T. S. Eliot's ability to hold down a job in the bank is modulated by his incapacity to handle a normal marriage. Nature may have been very wise in the niggardliness with which artistic gifts are distributed across the species, which then argues against aiming for breeding ourselves into a race of leonardian supermen. We need nice sturdy indifferent dachshunds if badger hunting is to continue, but still the aesthetic impulse is not be suppressed, and there remains a ground in fancy for the long low dog or the affectingly incompetent painter.

The fancy-breed view of the artist goes hand in hand with the standard view of art as essentially a disinterested activity and the appreciation of art itself as disinterested in turn, and where, in the routine taxonomies of our discipline, an essential contrast between the aesthetic and the practical is taken for granted. That art, hence the artist, should be gloriously useless, would not be an argument against breeding for the latter, since the impulses that make for fancy breeding are themselves traits of the human character with a grounding in the genetic material, and account for a main class of reasons for selecting mates, sites, forms of costume and shelter, for no reason more compelling than compliance with fancy. Museums merely enshrine practices which find their realization throughout civilization, in dog shows and beauty contests, rabbit fairs and flower expositions, and in iron pumping, crash diets, silicone implants, face-lifts, codpieces, plastic bangles, lace underwear, and shoulder pads. Counterparts to these are to be found throughout the zoosphere, and it is hard to insist on the inutility of fancy when it yields a class of reasons for action in a universe that would be starlingly indifferent without it. A scheme in which a face can launch a thousand ships is not evolutionarily insensitive to taste. The aesthete may himself be as unfit as the artist in the larger struggles for life, but the trait that is so remarkably developed in his case is as adaptive, at a lower degree of development, as the basset's ears are when not absurdly long: they may serve as furnishing stimuli which hold the hound's head at the optimal position for scenting. Everything fanciful has a utilitarian origin, or it would not have survived to be bred for.

But even if the artist were bred for purposes of utility because art itself is finally practical, he might for all that be eccentric, for just the reason that domestic economy favors specialization. Sheep are bred for wool or for mutton, and though dual-purpose breeds exist, it is as though nature exacts a cost in delicacy of taste in exchange for cashmere-quality fiber. And as there are human goals which call for long, as against short-haired fleeces, we may find that we have to sacrifice the meat to get what we want. So if we bred humans by the principles Darwin lays down in *Variations of Animals and Plants under Domestication*, we would have to weigh the costs of cultivating for art as against other human varieties, and balance the utility of art against other values of domestic reality. And there are, as we know, some deep and famous schedules of social stratification which would advise against breeding artists. Plato, whose generative program bears comparison with Piero's, saw problems enough in breeding for philosophers and warriors without contaminating the gene pool with the human-all-too-human, though the knowledge of breeding was sufficiently advanced for him to know that inborn dissimilarity among the members of a carefully selected variety is rarer and less marked than in groups where breeding would be left to aesthetic or dynastic criteria: in fact Plato saw in this the only prophylaxis against political degeneration. It is well known that artists were to be exiled, doubtless to keep artistic genes from also contaminating the severely husbanded pool, but this because Plato saw the products of artists as characteristically counterutilitarian and not just nonutilitarian, as he would have believed had he had the benefit of the Third Critique of Kant, which teaches that art is essentially a matter of fancy—of developing to the point of purposelessness traits which in the common human stock may have some residual purpose.

If there is reason to breed artistic talent out, on grounds of being subversive to platonic political economy, then there is reason to breed for artistic talent if and only if some political or social structure is imagined in which art plays some useful, or counterkantian, function better than anything else. This would be true even if, expectedly, the artist himself should be good for little beyond artmaking, on the model of the merino sheep of Spain, its fine, white, and abundant wool more than compensating for the fact that rack of merino is poor eating alongside the *mouton pré salé* of Brittany, whose wool is nothing to write home about. Of course it could all be nothing more than fancy, but my expectation is that the sponsor of this lectureship, for whom art is the chief agency of human evolution, had in mind something more useful than the evolution of connoisseurs and collectors, curators and critics, art fanciers who hand out the cups and commissions as their counterparts on panels of juries at pig displays and dog shows recognize the benign exaggerations of dab hands of the breeder's art.

It must have been an agony to racialists of the nineteenth and twentieth centuries that the offspring of blacks and whites, Brahmans and Sudras, goyim and Jews, should breed while the offspring of donkeys and horses were sterile. Pigmentation and facial type prevail through inbreeding over millennia, doubtless reinforced by fancy, and though black and white may seem morphologically more distant than whatever marks horses from donkeys, species are defined through reproductive isolation rather than morphological similarity. In fact it is known that these are genetically distinct, so that morphological differences are found within species, while morphologically similar species are intersterile. So racialists were obliged to fall back, like Plato, on eurgenic prohibitions, exile being the ancient form of what has come to be known as Final Solutions, and accept their conspecificity with their inferiors. Human breeders, in either sense of the term, have thus far been incapable of producing a novel heritable trait, and Darwin's audacious thought was that heritable traits evolve in a way altogether similar to the way in which desired traits are bred for in the barnyard. Reproductive isolation makes it sound almost analytic that this cannot happen, but the image was that branchings over vast millennia may cease being interfertile, though a million years is too short for this to happen. Most of what we know is inscribed in the fossil record.

I mention these familar things because, if art itself is to be a means to the further evolution of humankind, we cannot be talking about some new heritable traits, but about traits which have been in place for millennia. And for nearly as long as we have archeological records, there is evidence that something like artmaking has been part of the human phenotype, doubtless with a basis in the DNA whence the rest of what is distinctively human is encoded—the propensity to language, for example, if that is distinctively human. These are the traits we would breed for in my fanciful project of artificial selection of artists. Nevertheless, something has been left out of this picture, which is that the propensity to artmaking realizes itself in different ways at different times, so that the sequence of ways of artmaking itself seems to have an evolutionary structure, and this is not accounted for in Darwin's scheme, or not so far as I have been able to make out. Imagine an isolated hunter in some remote past era incising a bone with some lines which have little immediate to do with the purposes he has in mind with the bone itself: they are decorative, say, or rudimentarily pictographic. That incised bone becomes part of the environment and may become something against which another hunter exercises his own artistic impulses, modifying or merely repeating it. Over a stretch of time we can mark an evolution of sorts in the bone markings, so at the end point perhaps quite different traits are called upon to engage in artmaking than would have been required at an earlier stage—viz., suppose someone had added color. Artmaking and connoisseurship evolve together, and what we do and how we respond are very much a function of what our historical location in this process is. To the degree that art modifies the environment to which artmaking itself must adapt, then I suppose it would in a sense be true that art is a means for human evolution in a way which resembles the evolution of varieties or even the descent of species. Reasonable only, of course, because there is no modification of the genetic material, and if the institutions through which artmaking is encouraged and taught were erased, say by some historical catastrophe, we would in the next generation exercise or manifest our artmaking traits by scratching bone or piling stones. But the mediation of history and the evolution of institutions was not something to which Darwin paid great attention.

Darwin had the incredible, almost *übermenschliches*, courage to extend the theory of evolution to cover human beings: if evolution has taken place elsewhere in the universe, it must have taken place with us as well; and Darwin was tireless in exhibiting the commonalities, for example in the expression of emotions, between animals and ourselves. What he did not especially discuss was what made the theory of evolution itself historically possible at one time rather than another. Darwin was in many ways a genetic determinist, and pondered the differences between his brother and himself. His brother, Erasmus Alvey Darwin, was interested in art and literature rather than observing insects, and Darwin wrote in a famous passage that he "inclined to agree with Francis Galton in believing that education and environment produce only a small effect on the mind of anyone, and that most of our qualities are innate." Piero da Vinci might have been moved to the same reflections had Leonardo *due* turned out to be a businessman and womanizer. But what Darwin did not reflect on was the historical location of himself: he clearly would not have come up with the theory of evolution had he been born in some different time. Fifty years later, and it would long since have been discovered, if only by A. R. Wallace. Fifty years earlier, even had he a natural bent toward evolutionary thinking, he could hardly have come up with a theory into the historical explanation of which we have to take account of Sir Charles Lyell's *Principles of Geology* and Malthus's theory of population, which suggested the mechanism under which favorable traits are preserved. A theory that cannot account for its own emergence, if it *is* a theory of emergence, is seriously incomplete, but we can accommodate the theory of evolution to this task only by historicizing the concept of the environment and recognizing, with Wölfflin, that not everything is possible at every time, even when we are dealing with creatures who, like ourselves, have undergone no significant genetic modification from the time of our emergence.

Now if art is to be a means of human evolution, as David

Mandel wants to believe, it has to be in some way in which history itself is relevant, so that we, as it were, would be historically different persons in consequence of art at the end of the process than at the beginning. But that means that art itself must have a certain historical structure such that the changes it induces in us enter the history of art as determinants of its evolution. I do not want to say that something like this is not true, but if it is, then certain standard views of the historical transformation of art would have to be false.

Consider, for example, the deeply influential theory that art is mimesis, or that whatever else art may be it is centrally mimetic. It was Vasari's immense insight that mimesis has a history, and that if we examine the sequence of mimeses from Cimebue to Michelangelo, we have to admit that artists got better and better at it, so that there was an unmistakable progress in the conquest of visual appearances. Though he does not engage in counterfactual speculations, Vasari might have inferred that "education and environment" produce immense effects, since no one who painted at the beginning of the period would have painted as he did were he instead to have been born toward the end, even with the same innate endowment. This would be generally true: it is difficult to suppose Leonardo would have painted the Virgin and Saint Anne were he to have grown up in the East Village—if in fact one does grow up in the East Village—or that Rothko would have painted his vague moody rectangles in the ateliers of Louis XV. But let us stick with mimesis simply understood, where the effort is to present the eye with an array of stimuli to which the optical response is the same as it would have been to the array of visual stimuli presented by the reality we say the painting is of. If Vasari recognized that there is a history of this, Gombrich recognized what makes this history possible, and how long a road had to be travelled before artists got to be as good at it as legendarily they are supposed to be if they are to dupe real birds with painted grapes. Illusion gives us our criterion of success, and Gombrich insists, I believe correctly, that there was a long intervention of a process of making-and-matching, with certain points of profound breakthrough, such as the discovery of linear perspective (in historical truth I believe it was less the possibility of illusion than the demonstration that perception has a mathematical structure which would have been claimed as the real achievement of perspective.

But making is one thing and matching is another, and while the former has a history of the sort Gombrich describes, it is unclear that the latter does. It is said that there is no innocent eye, but in fact the eye is very innocent: visual perception may be among the modularities of mind, cognitively impenetrable, and indeed cognitive science has come forth with amazing demonstrations as to how little of learning enters into seeing, how much of it is native equipment. What is true is that the *hand* is not innocent, and if there were the institutional catastrophes I referred to, in which we were returned to a state of nature, we would have to learn to represent all over again, but we would see exactly as we do see: so matching does not have the history that making does, as may be evidenced by the observation that without the ability to match there would be no concept formation at all. Gombrich supports this with psychological exactitude: "even the crudely coloured renderings on a box of breakfast cereal would have made Giotto's contemporaries gasp." But just to the degree that the gasp testifies to surprise, there is an argument that while it took the whole history of representation from Giotto to the Wheaties box to learn to render that way, it took no history at all to see that way: the gasp would be due to the astonishment that the hand had caught up with the eye. So we may conclude that if art is supposed to have transformed human beings, the history of art cannot have been the history of illusion and the essence of art cannot be mimesis. It cannot because we are the same at the end of the progress as at the beginning, so that there has been no human evolution. Of course there was an evolution in dexterity, and this might be said to induce a certain selection procedure in that more and more skill is demanded of artists toward the end of the progress than at the beginning: we might suppose that in order to enter the history of art at the beginning, not very much by way of mimetic power would be demanded, but as the struggle for illusion continued, those with lower degrees of talent would be selected out, and more and more virtuosity would be favored by the process. The history of art would be like the history of performance in music, or like the history of athletics, where contenders enter at more and more exacting levels of reflex. That is a different story from the one I am seeking to tell, though it is worth dwelling on the thought that as the nature of art itself is reconceived, a very *different* type of artist gets selected for and the traits that earlier gave his possessor a serious advantage prove to be irrelevant to survival under the new order. It was leveled at the ghastly Whitney Biennial of 1985 as a criticism that the artists did not know how to draw. But drawing skill may have become quite irrelevant to art as it has evolved today. So let us turn to another model of the history of art.

A crux in the long theoretical litigation over the innocence of the eye has been the status of linear perspective: does it represent the way the eye sees, or do we see in perspective because of it, our ways of representing having entered the history of perception which proves cognitively penetrable after all? There is a historical view of perspective which is neutral in a way to this controversy, namely that perspective is a kind of symbolic form, which of course was Panofsky's view, set forth in a difficult and perhaps not fully determinate paper. I say it is neutral because it is consistent with it being a symbolic form that should also exemplify the way the eye perceives: it would just be that the culture in which it was discovered, perhaps the only culture in which it was discovered, had decided to make the way we actually see symbolic. Panofsky's theory of iconology was that there is some underlying structure in every culture which determines the culture to symbolize the world, or represent it, in different ways, and the task of the iconologist would then be to identify this iconogen, as we may call it, and show how everything that defines the culture is a variant on it. His book on the Gothic, for example, seeks for an iconogen whose natural exemplification's were in Gothic architecture and scholastic philosophy, these being among its symbolic forms: but doubtless there are other symbolic forms in that culture to be explained through the same iconogen. In the Renaissance, there was a different iconogen, and perspective was one of its major exemplifications. It would fit with the ideology of the Renaissance that it should enoble the human eye by setting up what pertained to it as how its members believed themselves to be: and this would be exemplified throughout the culture, in styles of artchitecture, politics, history, and poetry.

On Panofsky's view, never so far as I know quite worked out in any great detail, the history of art would be the history of symbolic forms, which in effect means the history of iconogens, each generating a different set of symbolic forms. This would be a deeply discontinuous theory of the history of art, by contrast with the deeply progressive and hence continuous theory subscribed to by Vasari. Vasari saw only the one iconogen—naturalistic representation—but saw it as having its ups and downs from ancient times to his own, with a very dismal dip in what he thought of as the dark ages. But Panofsky sees the periods as incommensurable: we do not do well what the medievals did badly, but each of us does different things, with very different meanings and calling for very different skills. Someone left over from the building of Chartres might not have to learn a lot of new skills to participate in the building programs of Florence or Rome, but he would have to learn a new way of seeing things and hence a new way of judging, which means that judging across iconogenic periods would be illegitimate.

There is a sense in which symbolic forms are themselves the symbolic form of Panofsky's period, as of our own. For there can be no question but that whereas theorists used to see continuity, we see discontinuity everywhere. Think of the history of science, as seen by Thomas Kuhn, as the succession of paradigms each generating a different style of normal science. Think of the archeology of knowledge, as practiced by Foucault, where there are such deep incommensurabilities between the way we see things as compared with earlier periods that the very possibility of truth dissolves away, leaving only room for the possibility of domination and power. Even the theory of evolution today has this structure. Whereas it used to be that when there were discontinuities in the fossil record, scientists would say the record was incomplete, and look for what were called missing links, the new evolutionists say instead that the record is complete: it is evolution that is discontinuous. The theory of punctuational equilibrium represents evolution as a sequence of catastrophic flips, as it were, abrupt shifts to a new level, after which there is no change to speak of until the next one. And just as perspective could be at once exactly descriptive of optical processes *and* a symbolic form, symbolic forms could be at once symbolic forms and the way history actually moves. To the degree that there is continuity, we are in the equilibrium period. But there is no continuity between the kernels of the different periods and cultures with their own array of symbolic forms. Iconology, as the pursuit of iconogens, is a formula for what I have elsewhere called "deep interpretation," that form of interpretation which seeks for structures which underlies the surfaces of culture and which its various symbolic forms express. Conceivably, all human practices under the sway of a given such structure are its symbolic forms: and when it changes, everything changes. And these "deep changes" are reflected at the surface of art history as the intuitive divisions between stylistic periods— Mannerism, Baroque, and the like.

I want to observe at this point that if there is anything to this model of art history, art itself is too epiphenomenal to a major instrument of evolutionary change; and so for the support of Mandel's thesis, it is little better than the familiar progressive model of art history, which assumes the antecedent structures of perception. This is because art, as a symbolic form, is on the surface rather than an ingredient in the internal deep structures which art expresses or, to use Schopenhauer's terminology, which art objectifies. Whatever may have been the kernel of the medieval period, it was objectified by philosophy and by the semiotics of social stratification as much as by architecture and, for all I know, systems of taxonomy and astrology. Perspective may have been a symbolic form of the Renaissance, but costume and city planning and perhaps certain views of history of the sort we find in Vasari might be other symbolic forms. So its art may be among the ways that a culture represents its inner life to its members—but for just this reason it is not transformative at the level at which we would want to speak of evolution. Causality takes place at the level to which deep interpretation takes us, from kernel to kernel as it were, and on this Panofsky had, I think, little to say, as though he was sufficiently taken in by his schematism of catastrophic changes to have supposed that his was only another one, a way of reading the world with no objective basis, so that there would be no hope of an explanation. Explanation would *anchor* symbolic forms to reality in such a way as to draw the sting of relativism from Foucault's philosophy: something I believe he would have been unable to tolerate. Someone anxious to deny the existence of solid ground will not be anxious to find a place to stand. But if the theory of punctuational equilibrium can at once exemplify the way we look at the world and be true, it is possible to insist on all the differences Foucault has revealed to us and then press for an explanation. In the case of art, that would be a *Kunstwissenschafft* rather than *Kunstgeschichte:* a theory of art rather than a phenomenology of stylistic change. And except for marxism, there are very few candidates for this role: but it was precisely one of the tenets of historical materialism that art is in the superstructure rather than in the base of deep historical change, and so not deeply transformative in its own right at all.

There is a third model of history, one which incorporates features of the other two, which was set forth by Hegel, and which I sought to vindicate in a certain sense in my essay "The End of Art." This is a kind of cognitive model, and characteristically of Hegel's idealism, the causalities of history are in effect the causalities of thought, which he interpreted romantically, as a process of inquiry and investigation, rather than classically, as the rehearsal of eternal logical forms. Hegel saw history pretty much as the effort to come to an understanding of its own processes: an unconscious effort to break through to consciousness of itself. In effect, he saw history as a drive to form its own philosophy, which he congratulated it for having attained in his own work: as though history really had come to its fulfillment in him. What is striking in Hegel's thought is that art, not always but at a certain stage, played a central transformative role in this process. At that point, art moves from its passive role as symbolic form, marking as it were a stage of thought taking place at another level, and becomes a force in history.

Bizarre as Hegel's theory is, in every possible respect, there is a reversal in the direction of causality, and the epiphenomenal and passive become causal and active—when Rosenkranz and Guildenstern become the pivots of a history in which they had otherwise been only very distant participants. This, if true in fact, would not vindicate Mandel's thesis in its general form: art would not have been the chief means of human evolution; but there would be a historical moment in which it was that. Of course none of this takes place at the genetic level, but rather at the level of thought. Art, through its own internal development, reached a stage where it contributed to the internal development of human thought to achieve an understanding of its own historical essence. When that happened, one could no longer think of art as one had thought of it before: but neither could one practice it as one had practiced it before, which is part of what I had in mind by the idea of art having come to an end. It has come to an end in that we cannot think about it in the same terms as before: and a deep transformation of thought such as this is exactly a shift in evolution; unlike perception, thought is not modular. And it is a transformation of thought that art made happen.

My sense is that this profound change takes place with the historical shift to modern art, roughly near the turn of this century. *Modern art* is not a temporal indicator, meaning what is happening now—as may be supported by the consideration that modern art is over with, save as a manner, and postmodern art is taking place now. No: "Modern Art" refers to a stylistic period, like Mannerism or Baroque. But the shift into the period it names is not just another shift to a new period: it is a shift to a new kind of a period. It marks a kind of crisis. In Sartre's beautiful ontology, there is a moment when the *pour soi*, as he terms it, which up to then had been invisible to itself, a pure nothingness, becomes, abruptly, an object for itself, at which point it enters a new stage of being. Less climactically, there is a stage in the history of each of us when we become objects for ourselves, when we realize we have an identity to inquire into: when we see ourselves rather than merely see the world. But we also recognize that becoming conscious of ourselves as objects is not like becoming conscious of just another object: it is a new kind of object, a whole new set of relationships, and indeed all the old relationships and objects are redefined. In modern art, art became an object for itself in this sense or something like it. I am incidentally impressed with the fact that the shift from the first to the second model of art history coincides, historically, with the shift from premodern to modern art.

The philosophical story is roughly as follows. Let us suppose that from the time of Giotto to roughly the end of the nineteenth century, there was a gradual progress in the con-

quest of visual appearances, in the eliciting of illusion, granting that this progress was marked by various punctuations
and long periods of equilibrium. Even Impressionism is part
of this history, the Impressionists having made certain discoveries about the color of shadows, about the nature of
color, about how patches at near glance fuse into forms at a
distance. Nevertheless there were certain inherent limits to
this, and my argument has been that the advent of motion
picture technology showed that the limits could not be broken within the standard possibilities of painting and sculpture. At this point, the progress was to be carried forward by
a new medium altogether, and one which, just because it
could show movement, could also better achieve the representation of narrative than painting ever could hope to do:
painting supposed that observers already knew the stories,
biblical, classical, Shakespearean: but telling new stories was
another matter altogether, and in any case required immense
cooperation on the part of the audience. Movies could address themselves directly to the narrative centers of the audience's minds: very simple, even illiterate audiences could
understand the stories they were shown. It has often been
remarked that the intellectual level of moving pictures was
exceedingly primitive at a time when that of art was very
high: when Cubism was being worked out, the movies
showed people falling in puddles and receiving custard pies
in their faces. But this would be wholly explicable if, as I
believe, painting and sculpture realized that they had to define their nature if they were to continue. And this is the
crisis to which I refer: paintings and sculpture, as art, become objects for themselves, and the further evolution of art
could henceforward take place only on the level of philosophy. Modern art is philosophy in the medium that up to then
had been treated as transparently as consciousness is supposed to have been in traditional theories of the mind. Locke
once wrote, beautifully, of the understanding which "like the
eye, whilst it makes us see and perceive all other things,
takes no notice of itself; and it requires art and pains to set it

at a distance, and make it its own object." Painting, similarly, made us see and perceive all things within its limits: but when those limits were themselves perceived, art became its own object in a philosophical move that almost exactly recapitulates what Hegel calls Absolute Knowledge, where the gap between subject and object is overcome. Of course self-consciousness came to cinema as well, preeminently in the work of Vertov, but it was not an internal necessity but as a philosophical application through which this transpired.

I think of iconology, as programmaticized by Panofsky, as a response, on the level of theory, to this crisis. Panofsky was liberated by art to the insight that optical deception was not essential to art only because art itself had to dissociate itself from this if it was to have a future: it had to insist that it itself was only incidentally representational, for otherwise it was defeated by moving pictures. So Panofsky insists that perspective is less a representational enhancement than *a* way of ordering the world, to be set as an equal alongside other ways of ordering it, none better or worse than any other. And so others would conclude that there is no progress at all, but that kind of relativism of symbolic forms—the art of X, of Y, of Z—we find displayed side by side in the pluralistic corridors and galleries of our museums. But there was progress, brilliant progress: it was the progress from art to philosophy that Hegel had described so powerfully in his astonishing lectures on the fine arts. It was a progress of cognition, from one level to another, where cognition became its own object.

Early modernist art required of its practitioners a finding of their own way, and every work and movement was a kind of theory in action. As I see it, there were two main moves. The one was to deny that the essence of art lay in representation at all, which led in a few years, inevitably, to abstract art and formalistic aesthetics, which remains so central a feature of modernism. The other, which on the surfaces of works would have been difficult to distinguish from abstraction, retained the criterion of representationality, but insisted that it was the task of art to represent a higher reality than the optical, which connected art to an ancient misprision of the senses, part of the fateful platonic syndrome of western civilization, and to all sorts of new realities, such as the fourth dimension and such occult realities that obsessed modernists in this period. By relating to a higher reality than cinema could show, locked as it was in the physiology of motion detection, this was a move to trump its oppressor by brilliant outflanking. Cubists are located somewhere in between, with some of the lesser Cubists clearly seized by occult aspirations. I think we cannot overestimate the extent to which early modernists were possessed by a sense of higher realities, which painting could serve as a bridge to, and this made painting a highly transformative activity: one need but reflect on the mission for art projected by Kandinsky's essay on spirituality. It was an era whose chief artistic product, I believe, was the manifesto. And if I may bite conjecturally the hand that feeds me, the thesis that art is a means, even *the* means, to the further evolution of humanity belongs to this stage of thought. The thought was irresistible that art revealed a higher reality to which we would become greater and more spiritual in consequence of adapting to it.

Even when it retained its cathexis to perceptual reality, however, illusionism was rejected by the early modernists in their quest for self-definition, and of course perspective would have been the first thing to go: its absence from the work of Van Gogh and Rousseau made their work difficult to grasp until it was realized what the significance of its absence was, and I surmise that until it had been abandoned by artists it could not have occurred to Panofsky that persepctive itself was but a symbolic form: for in a sense its absence or distortion had themselves become a charged symbolic form, leading to the inescapable view that how the artist orders the world is very much up to him. The structures of the second model of art history, in brief, became visible only with the demise of the first model. And we today are living with the consequences of this model in the pluralisms that do not only characterize projects of art making: they define contemporary, or post modernist, culture in morality, politics, theories of history, even science if we subscribe to the most radical philosophies of science abroad today. We have entered an intellectual Land of Coquaine, where, as Hegel would describe it, all are free.

Nowhere, it seems to me, is this license more evident than in the practice of criticism, where we badly need the phrase "making criticism" to correspond to "making art." Not long ago a major theorist raised a scandal by suggesting that criticism was where creativity was truly to be found, and that art in a way existed to make criticism possible. But in fact the distinction between art and criticism gives way when the critic is free to say anything at all, as so much of criticism seems to be. But this is only one of the boundaries erased in postmodernism: others are those between artist and dealer, dealer and critic, gallery and street, let alone the old generic divisions among the arts. We have entered a period of art so absolute in its freedoms that art seems but a name for an infinite play with its own concept: as though Schelling's thought of an end state of history as "a universal ocean of poetry" were a prediction come true. Artmaking is its own end in both sense of the term: the end of art is the end of art. There is no further place to go.

No further place, that is, with art itself, for which there is now but one unending Whitney Biennial. It is, howver, one thing to play with a concept and another to analyze it, and what art, in bringing us to this final stage of understanding, has done, has been to demonstrate that the instances which fall under the concept are so various that it would be a deep mistake to identify art with any of them. Having reached this point, where art can be anything at all, art has exhausted its conceptual mission. It has brought us to a stage of thought essentially *outside* history, where at last we can contemplate the possibility of a universal definition of art and vindicate therewith the philosophical aspiration of the ages, a definition which will not be threatened by historical overthrow.

Pluralism and relativism are philosophies which take their stimulus from the dizzying array of cases. A universal definition of art, a closed theory, must allow for an openness in the class of cases, and must explain this openness as one of its consequences. Postmodernism is the celebration of openness. The end of postmodernism lies in its explanation.

For the indefinite future, art will be post-historical artmaking. It would be inconsistent with this insight into history to look for a further history for it. Now the further history is for philosophy to take, and unlike art, philosophy is something that will have no post-historical phase, for when the truth is found, there is nothing further to do. Nothing could be more dismal to contemplate than philosophizing without end, which is an argument that philosophy is not art and that pluralism is a bad philosophy of philosophy.

My aim has been to show how art has been the means to philosophy at both ends of its history, but here, especially, when in transforming itself into its own object, it transformed the whole of culture, making a final philosophy possible, it served as an evolutionary means of the highest sort. Asked what artist we might breed for, my answer is, those with the keen sense of play that survival in the artworld now demands. The more important question is what philosophers to breed for, and my answer is, those who can give us the philosophy that art has prepared us for. I am but their prophet.

Index